A Brief History of Gresham College 1597–1997

Richard Chartres and David Vermont

GRESHAM
COLLEGE

This edition first published in 1998

Copyright ©1997 Gresham College

British Library Cataloguing in Publication Data
A Catalogue record for this title is available from the
British Library

ISBN 0 947822 16 X

Typeset in 11/14pt Garamond

Designed and Produced by Robin Ollington and Frank Lee

Printed in England by St Edmundsbury Press Ltd.
Bury St Edmunds, Suffolk

A Brief History of Gresham College 1597–1997

Thomas Gresham 1544 portrait at Mercers' Hall
Reproduced by kind permission of the Mercers' Company

FOREWORD

This survey of the history of the College in its quatercentenary year not only discharges a debt of piety but also concentrates the mind on the prospects for Gresham College in its fifth century. Like some mythical island, the College has emerged from the engulfing waters and disappeared again on several occasions. Each time very similar questions have arisen. What were the Founder's intentions and how can they be honoured in vastly changed circumstances? What kind of educational constituency should the Professors of the College seek to address? Would it be wise for the College to associate itself with complementary institutions? Who should in the last analysis make decisions about these matters and how can a consistent policy be developed?

The following sketch is intended to be a small contribution to this debate while telling the story of the College in the past four hundred years. The account of the first three hundred years is a revised version of a series of three lectures delivered at Gresham College in 1992 when I had the honour to be Gresham Professor of Divinity. The lectures made no pretensions to be a work of profound or original scholarship and the extent of my debts to others is indicated in the bibliography. The increasing press of business which followed my appointment first to the Bishopric of Stepney and then, in the footsteps of the early seventeenth century Professor of Divinity, George Montaigne, to the see of London conspired to delay the publication of these lectures. They would never have seen the light of day at all, had it not been for the encouragement of the Council of the College and in particular of Maggie Butcher, the Academic

Registrar. I am also grateful to the ever helpful staff of the Guildhall Library and its Archives.

The story of the past 100 years is the work of David Vermont, sometime Chairman of the College Council, who has played such a large and positive role in the changes of recent years. The achievement for the first time in the history of the College of the status of a legal entity in December 1994 has laid the foundation for a hopeful passage into the next century.

The public reputation of the College today probably stands higher than for many years past and this is thanks to the continued commitment of the Corporation of the City of London and the Mercers' Company. Thomas Gresham appointed these two bodies jointly to oversee his will. It is a tribute to the continuities of English public life that four centuries later they are still discharging their trust.

This Brief History is dedicated to the memory of Professor Peter Nailor, first Provost of the revivified Gresham College of recent years and himself an alumnus of Mercers' School. It fell to him to give the Inaugurating Lecture in 1991[1] when the College moved to its new home in Barnard's Inn, a new beginning that was followed only too soon by his illness and death. May he rest in peace and rise in glory!

+ Richard Londin:

---

1. See Appendix I for text of Lecture.

THE FOUNDER

If to be rich and to be learn'd
Be every Nation's cheifest glory
How much are Englishmen
      concern'd,
Gresham, to celebrate thy story
Who built th'Exchange t'enrich the
      Citty
And a Colledge founded for the
      witty.
*(A Restoration 'Ballad of Gresham
Colledge' ascribed to Joseph Glanvill.)*

Sir Thomas Gresham, the subject of this Restoration encomium, was born in 1519 into a dynasty of merchants. His father, Sir Richard Gresham, served as Lord Mayor of London in 1537 and both Greshams were involved in doing business with the Low Countries, the most significant area for English overseas trade for much of the sixteenth century. Sir Richard was the first Gresham to be inspired by the example of the Bourse in Antwerp and to contemplate a similar provision for the merchants of London. The even ampler means of his son Thomas brought this project to fruition thirty years later. The history of 'th'Exchange t'enrich the Citty' is to be found in Dr. Ann Saunders's 1997 publication *The Royal Exchange*.

The Greshams were a family long settled in Norfolk, a county dominated in the sixteenth century by the cloth trade, and their name is famously perpetuated in Holt by Gresham's School, founded, however, not by our Thomas but by his uncle Sir John Gresham.

In his youth, according to Dr. Gaius, Thomas Gresham was a gentleman pensioner of Gonville Hall, Cambridge but, as was frequently the case in those days for those not destined for ordination, he left without proceeding to a degree. In 1543, he was admitted to the Mercers' Company and the following year, at the age of twenty-five, he married a young widow, Anne. Her first husband, William Reade, also a merchant, had died earlier in the year.

Until 1549, when Sir Richard Gresham died, Thomas was occupied in the family business. His significant public career followed the financial crisis of 1551. Between May and August of that year there was a debasement of the coinage, the intrinsic value of which was reduced by half. Before this there had already been signs of a slump in cloth exports. The Antwerp market was nearly saturated and the effect of the monetary changes was to increase the relative cost of English cloth, and this further depressed demand.

In these difficult circumstances, Thomas Gresham was appointed 'King's Merchant' or Royal Agent in Antwerp. He retained the post continuously for sixteen years, surviving three changes of regime and three 'settlements' of religion. He seems to have inclined to the reformed side in the religious controversies of the day, but men of talent - not least in his specialised field - were in such short supply that he was found to be indispensable, even by the ministers of Queen Mary.

His main business was to manage the royal debt and his achievement was, as S.T. Bindoff succinctly remarked, to realise that 'credit rests on confidence and confidence rests on punctual repayment'. Gresham's Law that 'bad money tends to drive out good' is part of his legacy to the development of economics. Under his management, English royal credit came to stand so high that Mary and

Elizabeth could borrow more cheaply in Antwerp than the rulers of the Netherlands themselves.

Gresham made other contributions to the trade and commercial policy of Tudor England. Much of the import as well as export trade when he was appointed 'King's Merchant' was in the hands of the merchants of the Hanseatic League, operating from their base within the City of London at the Steelyard which stood on the site now occupied by Cannon Street Station. Gresham was influential in securing the cancellation of the privileges of the Hanse merchants and this opened the way to securing a closer regulation of the trade between England and the Low Countries. These trade controls were manipulated with a beneficial impact on rates of exchange.

Using the argument of the benefits of trade control, Gresham not only pressed for a trade monopoly to be granted to the Merchant Adventurers' Company of which he was a member, but he also advocated a concentration of power within the company in the hands of an oligarchy of the more substantial merchants.

At the same time Gresham, by now the Queen's Agent, supported an increase in customs duties which had the effect of confirming the Crown's financial interest in a flourishing but well regulated cloth trade. The increase in duties was secured in 1557 and by 1564 the Merchant Adventurers' Company was reconstituted on oligarchic lines. Gresham's whole programme had been adopted.

When Gresham began his career, England was something of a cultural backwater. As a resident for many years in Antwerp, one of the most significant commercial and political centres of contemporary Europe, Gresham was aware, as few of his fellow countrymen could be, of developments on the Continent. At the same time, as a successful man of affairs, from a merchant dynasty, he was well placed to know and deplore the relative scarcity of able professionals and skilled people of every kind in mid-Tudor England.

No doubt, like other Tudor patriarchs, Sir Thomas would have passed the bulk of his estate to his son and heir Richard, had not the boy died in 1564 shortly before attaining manhood. Gresham's natural daughter Anne, who married Francis Bacon's elder half-brother Nathaniel, also died before her father, and so when Thomas Gresham came to make his will in 1575 he was free, having made provision for his wife, to consider other ways of disposing of his vast fortune.

An epistle in Latin dated 15 March 1575 (New Style) from Richard Bridgewater, the Public Orator at Cambridge, suggests that it may have been Gresham's first intention to finance a new hall at Cambridge and that he had promised £500 for the purpose.

In the event, in his will dated 'the 20 day of *May*, in the seaventeenth yere of the raigne of our soveraigne lady Queene *Elizabeth*' (1575), a College in the City of London was envisaged. In addition to a number of bequests to the poor and to prisoners, one part of the revenues of the Royal Exchange property was given in trust to the Lord Mayor and Corporation, with another 'moiety' entrusted to the Mercers' Company for the purpose of establishing and supporting Gresham College.

The College was intended to be supplied with seven Professors in subjects selected by Gresham, with a bias towards those areas of study relevant to the City context. The Corporation was to have the nomination of four of the Professors: in Divinity, Astronomy, Geometry and Music. The Mercers' Company was to have the appointment of the Professors in Law, Physic and Rhetoric.

The inclusion of Astronomy in the list of lectureships is

particularly significant. It is noteworthy that Gresham assigned importance to this subject and to Geometry at a time when no such Chairs had been established at either Oxford or Cambridge. It is tempting to think that this innovation was connected with discoveries in this field in Gresham's own lifetime and, in particular, with the publication in 1543 of Copernicus's work on the heliocentric system. R.S. Westman's research into the diffusion of Copernican thinking in Europe, however, establishes that natural philosophers were slow to accept Copernicus in his entirety. He says that by 1600 in all of Europe there could not be found 'more than ten thinkers who chose to adopt the main claims of the heliocentric system'. Bacon for one remained unconvinced.

The scholars installed in these lectureships were to have stipends of £50 each, paid in equal portions on the feast of the Annunciation and at Michaelmas. This was generous provision for the time and exceeds the remuneration assigned by Henry VIII to the Regius Professors in the ancient universities. In addition, the Professors were to be given apartments in Gresham's mansion in Bishopsgate.

This great house, which was on the site now occupied by the NatWest Tower, was to be the base for the College until well into the eighteenth century. A fine engraving of the College was drawn by George Vertue for John Ward's book of 1740, *Lives of the Professors of Gresham College,* and it shows the disposition of the lodgings for the various Professors as they were in the mid-eighteenth century. Further details about the house and its layout can be found in Dr. Ann Saunders's contribution to the Society of Renaissance Studies Symposium on Gresham College, the proceedings of which are to be published shortly.

In line with the regulations obtaining at the ancient

universities, Sir Thomas also laid down in his will that 'none shall be chosen to read any of the said lectures so long as he shall be married, or be suffered to read any of the said lectures after that he shall be married'.

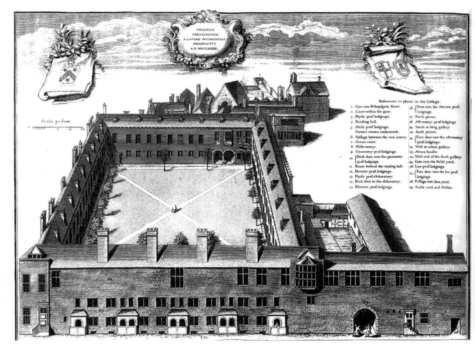

Engraving by George Vertue of Gresham College, looking east, showing the entrance in Old Broad Street, from John Ward's Lives of the Professors of Gresham College *(1740)*

 The will was signed and sealed with Gresham's device of the grasshopper four years before the great merchant died in November 1579. The Fugger Newsletter for the month reported that there was 'fearful rough weather' in England with 'rain heavy snow and unusual cold such as

has not been experienced for sixty years'. Holinshed's *Chronicle* records that 'on Saturday the 21st November 1579, between six and seven o'clock in the evening coming from the Exchange to his house in Bishopsgate Street, he suddenly fell down in his kitchen and being taken up he was found speechless and presently dead'. He was sixty.

Whereas previous generations, particularly in his own City of London, had regarded Gresham as not only a prodigious benefactor but also a hero, a fitting subject for the idealised statue on the Holborn Viaduct, there is now a disposition to be cynical about his character and motivation. It is suggested that his ability to prosper under very different regimes lays him open to the charge of being unprincipled and motivated chiefly by gain, and that his benefactions reflected a preoccupation with his reputation.

Although, like his friend and ally William Cecil, he certainly inclined to the Reformed side in religion, he was no enthusiast. As a merchant, and like Queen Elizabeth herself, he was interested in some kind of religious settlement which might promise a stable business environment. He had much experience of the destruction which could flow from religious broils, and his letters on his last visit to Antwerp in March 1567 were taken up with the loss of life and confusion which attended a serious clash between Protestant and Catholic forces in the city.

Gresham's precise intentions in founding his College must remain obscure since even near contemporaries found it difficult to articulate his mind. It is undeniable however that, as a merchant who knew the value of accurate and timely intelligence, he would not have been the only one to have regretted the comparative lack of provision in England for the scientific study of subjects like navigation and ways of diffusing knowledge useful to the mariners and traders who thronged the streets and quays of the City. In the very year that the College finally began its work, Richard Hackluyt, in the Epistle Dedicatorie to the revised edition of his *Principal Navigations*, lamented the lack of anything in England to match the institution by Charles V of the lectures in navigation, 'which is read to this day in the Contractation house of Sivil', the centre of the trade with the Indies. Gresham is commended, 'who being but a merchant hath founded so many chargeable lectures, and some of them also which are mathematicall tending to the advancement of marine causes'. Hackluyt's message to the Lord High Admiral, whom he is addressing, is 'go and do thou likewise'.

Much was to be gained by situating a College in the very centre of the traffic between practice and reflection. Thomas Gresham may have seen the potential without having a very precise notion of how his creation might develop. It was, after all, a novel educational concept in ways besides its location.

The College was obviously intended to be easy of access to those who might be qualified by experience but who did not possess the formal learning necessary to take advantage of the courses at the ancient universities. This was the significance of the debate about whether the principal medium of instruction at the College should be Latin (the international language of learning and scholarship) or the vernacular.

It was also clear that the lectures were to be free. The intention that they should be is laudable, but history might have been very different if the Professors had been able to charge fees rather than receive stipends. There would have been from the beginning less of an incentive to concentrate on private pupils than on the public lecturing.

Dr. Johnson's opinion, according to Boswell, was that if the Gresham Professors had only been able to take sixpence a lecture from each scholar, then they would have been 'emulous to have had many scholars'.

These novelties, as well as the important question of how his College was to be governed and directed, were left to be determined by his trustees, and by the time they entered into their responsibilities Gresham's handsome memorial in St. Helen's, Bishopsgate was nearly twenty years old. If the College, like the memorial, was intended as a way of enhancing Gresham's posthumous reputation - his 'fame and good report in this transitory world' as his will declares - then we can be grateful for a social order in which the rich were convinced they could contrive such a reputation by conspicuous expenditure for the public good.

DAYSPRING MISHANDLED

It took nearly twenty years after his death for Sir Thomas's intentions with regard to his College to be put into effect. He had granted his wife a life interest in the income from the Royal Exchange which amounted to about £750 per annum, equivalent to perhaps £375,000 in today's money. Gresham notes in his will that 'I do wholly put my trust in her and have no doubt but she will accomplish the same accordingly and all other things as shall be requisite or expedient for both our honesties, fames and good report in this transitory world'.

Immediately after Gresham's death there was a legal challenge to some aspects of the will by Sir Henry Neville who, as son-in-law to John Gresham, Thomas Gresham's brother, was the nearest male heir. Although he received two Sussex manors, including delectable Mayfield, he was dissatisfied with his portion, and the matter was only finally resolved by a private Act of Parliament in 1581. Thereafter, Dame Anne Gresham lived on in comfortable retirement until her own death in 1596.

By the time that the bequest became operative, many of Gresham's closest collaborators had themselves died. His old ally Lord Burghley was still at the heart of national affairs, but those in the City and in the Mercers' Company who had the principal responsibility for bringing the new College into being only had a dim idea of the Founder's intentions and the way in which he wanted his College to be governed.

The debate which followed has been unravelled by Dr. Ian Adamson in his reconstruction of the early history of Gresham College. All subsequent accounts have been dependent on Adamson's pioneering work.

One matter upon which Sir Thomas's will was clear was the right of appointment to the seven lectureships which he vested in the Corporation and the Mercers' Company, and so the Trustees set about recruiting the first Professors. Already, on 30 November 1596, the Lord Mayor had received a letter from the Queen desiring the post of Professor of Music for Dr. John Bull of Her Majesty's Chapel Royal. No doubt anxious not to lose control of the situation, the Lord Mayor at the beginning of 1597 wrote to the governing bodies of Oxford and Cambridge inviting two nominations for each of the lectureships.

This caused some perturbation at Cambridge where Dr. Jegon, the Vice-Chancellor, expressed some anxiety in a letter to his Chancellor and Gresham's old friend, Lord Burghley. Was there not a danger that promising young scholars would be attracted to the new institution in London rather than choosing to study in Cambridge? Perhaps also, academic memories being long, they remembered at Cambridge that Sir Thomas's original intention had been to benefit his old Alma Mater.

In the event, the first Gresham Professors were entirely drawn from Oxford and Cambridge. The three Oxford graduates were Edward Brerewood in Astronomy, Matthew Gwinne in Physic and Caleb Willis in Rhetoric. The Cambridge men were Anthony Wotton in Divinity, Henry Briggs in Geometry and Henry Mountlow in Law. Dr. Bull, the Professor of Music, Queen Elizabeth's candidate, held degrees from both universities.

Inaugural lectures were delivered at the end of 1597. Dr. Bull gave his inaugural on 6 October and, according to the Register of the Stationers' Company, it was printed by Thomas East. No copy, however, is known to have survived, although Dr. Burney, the eighteenth century music critic, claimed to have seen one.

These lectures justify the keeping of 1997 as the quatercentenary anniversary, but it seems that very little other teaching was done before the Trustees and the Professors fell into dispute. Adamson deduced this struggle from the existence of two early sets of College ordinances drawn up as part of the effort to translate Sir Thomas's rather vague intentions into detailed regulations for the life of his novel educational venture. According to Adamson, the Trustees envisaged the College 'as primarily a teaching institution, where the professors would constantly be in residence for personal consultation not just by other academics but by mariners, boat builders and the general public'.

The proposed syllabuses which have also survived reflect the different focus which might be expected in a London audience in contrast to the needs of undergraduates at the ancient universities. The emphasis on the application of learning was particularly marked in the new astronomy syllabus which was to be taught for its bearing on practical problems of geography and navigation. Although it has always been difficult to occupy competently and with integrity the marches between professional academic scholarship and the world of the practitioners, it remains a very important thing to attempt.

The Professors on the other hand struggled to reduce their teaching obligations and to introduce the restrictive practices with which they were already familiar at Oxford and Cambridge. The outcome of the conflict between the Trustees and at least five of the seven Professors was that the public teaching load was reduced for each lecturer from three hours a week spread over two days to two hours a week on just one day. Moreover, the lectures were confined to term time rather than being continued throughout the year as was the original intention.

The revisions in the ordinances did not affect the content of the proposed syllabuses but, since neither the first nor the second document seems to have been formally endorsed by the Professors, the precise content of their lectures, with the exception of the few published examples, must remain obscure.

In reflecting on this struggle, Mordechai Feingold in his significant book, *The Mathematicians' Apprenticeship,* proposed that, as a result of losing their struggle with the Professors, the 'trustees relinquished their function as agents for future initiative or reform'.

The Gresham Trustees did continue the struggle, but at a lower level. When Edmund Gunter died in 1626, a document was drawn up for the signature of his successor Henry Gellibrand. In particular, the Trustees imply their disapproval that Gunter, who as a former fellow of an Oxford College was ordained, had never given up his position as parish priest of St. George's, Southwark. His clerical duties seem to have absorbed a good deal of his time since Gellibrand had to promise that 'he would not hereafter take any calling or course unto him but apply himself wholly to this or else wholly leave the place'. He also promised 'to rest in the house as well in term as out of term whereby the more commodiously to give help to gents and mariners by private conference'.

The Trustees failed at the earliest period to develop a system of governance for the College which would put them in the driving seat. This was unsurprising since the expertise of the representatives of the Mercers' Company and the Corporation lay in other fields, and in any case they were men preoccupied with other matters, notably the management of the Royal Exchange.

The Professors also failed - or perhaps did not even try - to develop a College structure and, in particular, a corporate legal personality on the Oxbridge model which might have provided an alternative way of building an identity, with the possibility of a coherent response to changing circumstances. The problem was recognised at the beginning. There is an early paper printed by John Strype, the eighteenth century historian, in an appendix to his 1720 edition of Stow's *Survey of London*. Strype admits that he transcribed the paper rather hastily and is regrettably imprecise about its provenance, vaguely stating that it was 'found among many other original manuscripts sometime belonging to a great statesman in Queen Elizabeth's time'. It contains some proposals on College governance which would have given the College a more corporate identity. The author recognises 'forasmuch in every society, it is meet for the avoiding of confusion and emulation which may otherwise happen even among men of best quality, that certain orders should be observed in their open meetings and conversing together'. In consequence it is proposed that the first three and principal Professors in Divinity, Law and Physic are to be Presidents in succession. There are to be no lodgers and a common table.

It was not until 1994 that the College *per se* became a legal entity. Gresham's great house soon became principally a lodging in which the individual Professors went their own way and in many cases, far from residing, used their accommodation solely as a source of profit.

The struggle extended to the medium of instruction. Should the lectures be in Latin, the lingua franca of academic discourse in sixteenth century Europe, or should they be in the vernacular to cater for a less academic audience of city folk and especially mariners? The lecture series that do survive seem mostly to have been composed in Latin first, and this was obviously the way in which the Professors could best communicate with their peers both at home and abroad. An exception was made for the talented Dr. Bull who, although he had degrees from both Oxford and Cambridge, did not have a facility in Latin, and he was permitted to lecture only in English. This became traditional, but only for the Music Professor.

The document printed by Strype which reflects the Trustees' view suggests that if the lectures were all to be given in Latin then they 'in short time may become solitary'. Again however, the view of the Professors largely carried the day and it was agreed that the lectures should be in Latin, particularly in view of the large numbers of foreigners in London, but it was also agreed that there should be an epitome provided in English at another time. In Divinity the pattern was established of a Latin lecture at 9am on a Monday morning with an epitome in English at 3pm.

This debate was to rumble on for two centuries more. Strype, writing in 1720, after some years of argument about the way in which the Gresham bequests had been used, summarised the arguments for English. It would annoy the ancient universities less since it would tend to establish that the new institution was aiming at a new audience. There was also the fund-raising dimension, and there was the possibility that the use of English would increase the 'hope of contribution from the citizens'. Strype also urged that the use of English in the Divinity lectures would be best calculated to ensure that 'a true and grounded detestation of popery shall be bred in the Queen's subjects' hearts'.

From the beginning it was clearly the hope that the Divinity lectures would have a popular audience. Strype's early document asserts that they are to be given 'as may most tend to the glory of God and the common benefit of the people of this City (which we doubt not to be the principal end of the founder in the ordaining of the said lectures)'.

The same document does, however, enter a warning, which those familiar with the violent tone of many sixteenth century literary duels will appreciate, urging lecturers to distinguish between a proper academic approach and polemic. Lectures should not be 'enlarged or intermingled with exhortation being improper for a public lecture ... '.

Great attention has been properly paid to the teaching of science in the new institution, but some of the advice given to the Divinity lecturer illustrates the development of a distinctly 'academic' approach to the subject in an age of violent polemics.

The Divinity lecturer, in dealing with his contentious subject at a time when a trust existed in the City of London for the purchase of faggots for the burning of heretics, was instructed to 'endeavour to confirm the truth of doctrine now established in the Church of England and to confute the adverse part and with great conscience and circumspection to boulte out the true state of each controversy, specially drawn from the Council of Trent and the late writers of refined popery and to overthrow their false opinions first by scripture, then by consent of antiquity, and lastly by schoolmen and chief writers of their own side'. This appeal to antiquity as a complement to the scriptures was to become characteristic of the theology of the Church of England in the seventeenth century and gives it a flavour distinct from the work of Continental Protestants.

Feingold examines the scanty evidence for the early lectures at Gresham and the chance indications that have survived of the kind of response they drew and what kind of audience. He concludes that, as a teaching institution, with the possible exception of the Divinity Lectures, Gresham College was a failure. He also presents evidence pointing to the not unexpected conclusion that practical mariners and the like found, in the words of Arthur Hopton the mathematician in 1611, the lectures of 'great Scolers deeply seene in the theoreticall part' rather inaccessible. In consequence, attendance may well have been sparse, so confirming the lecturers that there was not sufficient demand to justify any very heavy teaching obligation.

No doubt this situation did damage the reputation of the College in London, and discontent with the way in which the Professors had reduced their teaching obligation rumbled on and surfaced in a pamphlet of 1647 preserved in the Guildhall Library. It is a quarto tract of eight pages published in the year of the fiftieth anniversary of the founding of Gresham College. It is entitled *Sir Thomas Gresham, His Ghost.* Facing the title page is a picture of Sir Thomas in a shroud holding aloft a blazing torch. He wears a grim aspect and the burden of the tract is that the Professors have perverted Gresham's beneficient intentions. They stand accused of being 'so superbiously pettish that they will resolve no Quaere that will advantage the Dubitour: nay they are come to that strain where they will do as they list; read whatt, when, how and where they list; and not at all if they list; and indeed they have their meanes for a song'.

This is not the whole story, however, and if Gresham College did not fulfil City expectations as a teaching institution, it rapidly acquired an international reputation as a place of academic research, with Professors who were in some cases working at the heart of the intellectual revolution of the seventeenth century. It is time to consider some of the early Professors and their contribution, particularly to the development of the mathematical sciences.

EARLY PROFESSORS OF
GRESHAM COLLEGE

A number of outstanding young scholars were nourished by the Gresham Foundation in the early years of the seventeenth century, and none more significant than Henry Briggs, the pioneer of logarithms. A good deal is known about Briggs's career, much of it helpfully assembled by Mordechai Feingold in *The Mathematicians' Apprenticeship*, a study of science, the universities and society in the period 1560-1640.

Before his appointment to the Gresham Chair, Briggs served as mathematical lecturer and examiner at St. John's College, Cambridge. After a number of years in London, Briggs was appointed in 1620 to the newly established Savilian Professorship in Geometry at Oxford.

Some of Briggs's lecture notes from the time that he was in Cambridge have survived. They reveal acquaintance with the works of Copernicus and form a part of the evidence for questioning the often repeated claim that science at the ancient universities was hardly taught at all, or if taught was confined within Aristotelian corsets. This thesis was proposed in a classical form by Christopher Hill in his book *The Intellectual Origins of the English Revolution*. His judgement was that 'the science of Elizabeth's reign was the work of merchants and craftsmen not of dons; carried on in London not in Oxford and Cambridge'.

The motive for the major scientific advances was held to be connected with mercantile enterprise and the need to solve practical problems of navigation, accounting, surveying and military engineering. In this context the foundation of Gresham College has been regarded as especially significant. While it would be implausible to discount the stimulus offered by the trading environment of London, too clear a contrast between the work being done at Gresham and studies in the clerically dominated ancient universities will not survive an analysis of the careers of the early Professors.

Briggs is a good example, for he, like all the Professors recruited by Gresham College, had affiliations with Oxford or Cambridge, and when opportunity presented itself moved back to the university. Edmund Gunter is another example. He has left a memorial in the field of surveying with 'Gunter's Chain' and is not forgotten by sailors who still refer to a 'Gunter Rig'. Prior to his appointment in 1619 to the Gresham Chair of Astronomy, he had been a Student of Christ Church. It is true, however, that there was a scarcity of well-remunerated science posts in the ancient universities, and the Gresham Chairs were a boon to the scientific community in the early seventeenth century.

Briggs was not only pivotal in relations within the British scientific community, he also kept up a lively exchange with scholars on the Continent. Although many of his letters have been lost, we know that he corresponded with Kepler about the application of logarithms to astronomical computations. Another of his correspondents seems to have been Lucas Holsten, the German chronologer and geographer, who from 1627 served as Keeper of the Vatican Library. Even in an age of religious conflict, scientists shared a common language, and Holsten wrote a commendation of Briggs's 1620 edition of Euclid.

Whatever the truth of the proposition that Gresham College did not fulfil the intention of its Founder nor his Trustees as a teaching institution, it was undeniably a most important centre of research in the first half of the seventeenth century, and a meeting place for many ingenious scholars who were associated with the Professors, though never directly members of the Foundation.

Among the more celebrated researchers, Sir Kenelm Digby lived at Gresham College from 1633-35. Following the death of his beloved wife Venetia, he retired to the College where, having equipped himself with 'a long mourning cloak, a high crowned hatt, his beard unshorne', he took on the appearance of a 'hermite'. During his stay 'he diverted himself with his chymistry and the professors' good conversation'.

He occupied five or six rooms under the lodgings of the Professor of Divinity which in the plan of 1740 are designated as the 'Physic prof. elaboratory'. Four of these rooms were converted into a laboratory in Digby's time, and it was here that he conducted his experiments into palingenesis - the attempt to 'revivify or resurrect plants and animals from their calcined ashes'. Jurassic Park, it will be remembered, was the result of similar experimentation.

To assist him in these experiments, Digby recruited the Hungarian alchemist Johannes Banfi Hunyades to serve as his operator. From other references it is clear that Hunyades also acted as an instructor in chemistry at Gresham and, despite the Trustees' hostility to lodgers, we must imagine the College community at this period being composed of a number of productive scholars in addition to the Professors.

The stimulus of the London location should not be underestimated as an influence on the eminence of Gresham College as a centre for research. Overseas competition with the Dutch, the Spanish and the Portuguese was a daily fact of life in the City as trade and colonising horizons expanded. There were indeed practical problems of navigation, astronomy and military engineering to solve under the stimulus of the very considerable profit which could be expected by the victor.

Some of these problems, like the nature of magnetism and the study of comets and eclipses, necessitated not only more accurate and sustained observation but also could only be explored with comparative observation from many points on the globe. Contact with seamen and correspondence with Continental scholars was part of the process, but so was the field expedition, and Gresham Professors took their share in this area of research also. Professor John Greaves for example set up no less than four observation posts in the Middle East in 1638 in order to observe the eclipse of the moon due for December of that year. He also arranged for the same phenomenon to be observed in England and in the Azores.

At a time when Galileo, condemned for his championship of the Copernican system, was under house arrest at the command of the Holy Inquisition, Greaves's researches into the heavens were conducted under the patronage of the scholarly William Juxon, Bishop of London. He wrote to the Gresham Committee in 1637 in support of John Greaves's expedition to the Middle East to make astronomical observations. 'This work I find by the best astronomers, especially by Ticho Brache and Kepler, hath been much desired as tending to the advancement of that science.'

Greaves had been appointed Gresham Professor of Geometry in 1630. William Laud was among his most significant patrons, and his journeys in the Middle East were partly undertaken in search of Arabic manuscripts for the Archbishop. Greaves was in Constantinople in 1638 in time for the strangling of its Patriarch, Cyril Lucaris, in June. In the Ottoman capital at the same time was the

Greek Patriarch of Alexandria, Metrophanes Kritopoulos, who had been a student at Gresham College in the 1620s, improving his English before going on to study at Oxford. It would have been surprising if they had not met, and in fact Greaves's next step was to go to Alexandria, both in pursuit of his scientific project and also as a collector of manuscripts.

Whilst in Egypt he surveyed and measured the pyramids, of which no satisfactory account had hitherto been published. While in the largest pyramid he made a measurement of 'the foot observed by all nations with his name John Gravius carved underneath it'.

On his return he was set to catalogue the Archbishop of Canterbury's coin collection which the harassed prelate had given to Oxford University and, in 1643, Greaves became Professor of Astronomy at Oxford.

He proposed a way of converting the country from the Julian to the Gregorian Calendar by omitting the Leap Year for forty years. Most of Catholic Europe had changed to the more accurate Gregorian Calendar in the 1580s, and Greaves's plan would have avoided the agitation which provoked rioters to demand, 'Give us back our eleven days' when Britain did finally make the change in 1752. In the mid-seventeenth century however, Calendar reform was a victim of fierce religious conflict between Catholics and Protestants, and Greaves's scheme was foolishly thought to reek of Popery.

In 1646, a year after his patron's execution in the Tower, Greaves's great book *Pyramidographia* was published.

But it was not only in the sciences that the College was in the European first rank. John Bull was thirty-five when appointed the first Gresham Professor of Music. He held the post for ten years. Before his Gresham period he had been a choirboy and organist at the Chapel Royal. Subsequently he was appointed organist at the Cathedral in Antwerp where Sir Thomas Gresham had laboured in the previous century. He was an important composer for virginals, and a virtuoso performer himself. He is regarded as one of the founders of the modern keyboard repertory.

Biographical sketches of some of the other seventeenth century Professors can be found in the work of John Ward, Gresham Professor of Rhetoric. In 1740 he published his *Lives of the Professors of Gresham College*. His own copy of the book was presented to the British Library, where it resides amended and enlarged with copious manuscript notes.

The brief lives of the Gresham Professors of Divinity illustrate among other things the impact of the patronage system on appointments to the College.

The first Professor of Divinity was Anthony Wotton of Eton and King's. He had been an unsuccessful candidate for the Regius Chair at Cambridge but was a noted scholar and controversialist. As a former Chaplain to the Earl of Essex he may be presumed to have had Puritan sympathies. These became manifest when he resigned from his chair upon marrying and became a preacher at All Hallows, Barking in 1604. He addressed an appeal to James I in the early days of his reign, praying that 'God open the eyes of the King that he may be resolved in the truth without respect of antiquity'. Wotton subsequently fell foul of the Bishop of London and was inhibited from preaching.

James I himself promoted the cause of William Dakins to succeed Wotton. Dakins had distinguished himself as a scholar both at Westminster School and Trinity College, Cambridge, and the intention was that he would be attached to the syndicate of divines assembled in Westminster to undertake the translation of the Pauline Epistles as part of the Authorised Version of the Bible. There is no denying the scholarly competence of a man like Dakins, but the appointment of George Montaigne in 1606 illustrates one of the difficulties of the new foundation. The method of presentation to the various chairs, in which preponderant influence was vested in those for whom academic considerations were not necessarily uppermost, led to a situation paralleled at the ancient universities yet in an aggravated form. The patronage system and the proximity of the court led to the appointment of candidates like Montaigne, who became a favourite of James I but was by no means an outstanding scholar.

Montaigne was a witty and accomplished courtier who had accompanied Essex on his expedition to Cadiz where he had distinguished himself with admirable but unclerical valour. He was to hold an astonishing succession of preferments as Dean of Westminster and then Bishop of Lincoln, London and Durham. Charles I did not share his father's good opinion of Montaigne whom he regarded, according to the seventeenth century historian Peter Heylyn, as 'a man unactive' and 'one that loveth his own ease too well to disturb himself in the concernments of the Church'. When the Archbishopric of York fell vacant, however, Montaigne wittily observed to the King, 'hadst thou faith as a grain of mustard seed, thou wouldest say unto this mountain (at the same time laying his hand upon his breast), be removed into that sea'. The King was amused and Montaigne was appointed.

He was followed by the first Gresham Professor of Divinity to be recruited from Oxford, William Osbolston. In another example of the continuities of London life, just as Osbolston preached the Archbishop Whitgift Founder's Day sermon to the pupils of the Whitgift School in Croydon Parish Church in 1613, the Gresham Professor of Divinity was invited back to perform the same duty in 1992. Not only that but the fee remained unchanged. Both Professors received 13s. 4d. from the Fishmongers' Company, a sum which in the early seventeenth century was intended to provide 'a competent dinner' for two score persons.

The appointment of Professors continued to mirror the rise and fall of the political barometer. Samuel Brooke, later Master of Trinity College, Cambridge, was a convinced Arminian and an ally of Bishop - later Archbishop - Laud. It was in a letter to Laud that Brooke spoke his mind on the dangers of Calvin's doctrine in unusually round terms. 'Their doctrine of predestination is the root of all Puritanism and Puritanism the root of all rebellious and disobedient intractableness in Parliament and of all schism and sauciness in the country; nay in the church itself.'

Richard Holdsworth was also an upholder of King and episcopacy, but after the moderate Calvinist school represented by Bishop Joseph Hall. His Gresham lectures in Latin, which seemed to enjoy some public success, were published in 1629. He also became a significant figure among the clergy of the City, being elected by them to the Presidency of Sion College which was founded in the late 1620s. Eventually Holdsworth returned to Cambridge as Master of Emmanuel and then Vice-Chancellor of the University.

In 1641 the relations between Crown and City were already very frail and there was a consequent diminution of court influence. Thomas Horton was appointed to the Professorship which he was to enjoy until after the

Restoration. He was an active supporter of the Presbyterian system of Church Order, a cause to which many City clergy at this period adhered. He was also the very first Gresham Professor to be married under a dispensation granted personally by Cromwell. This dispensation was initially renewed after the Restoration and Horton was nominated an assistant on the Presbyterian side at the Savoy Conference. He eventually conformed, however, to the 1662 Prayer Book and the re-established episcopal order of the Church and died as Vicar of Sir Thomas Gresham's old parish church, St. Helen's, Bishopsgate.

Passing the Professors of the first half century under review, it is clear that, at its best, Gresham's foundation could offer young scholars on their way up a well-paid exposure to the networks and stimulating themes of the rapidly expanding City of London. At its worst the College simply became a way of rewarding clients. There was enough to admire, however, for Sir George Buck, historian and Master of the Revels to James I, to describe the foundation in hopeful terms as 'a little university or academic epitome'. Buck's essay containing this phrase and entitled 'The Third Universitie of England' was published in 1615 as an appendix to Howe's edition of Stowe's *Survey of London*. It was destined to be taken up again and again, especially by nineteenth century would-be reformers of the College.

RESTORATION GRESHAM AND THE ROYAL SOCIETY

In 1657, while Thomas Horton was in his sixteenth year as Professor of Divinity, the young Christopher Wren - son of the ousted Dean of Windsor and then only twenty-five - gave his inaugural lecture as Professor of Astronomy. It is interesting to reflect on the fact that his father had been one of the chief contenders for the Astronomy post after the death of the first Professor, Edward Brerewood. Finding it difficult to pursue a remunerated scientific career, he took his BD in 1620 without, however, abandoning his interest in science.

In his lecture, Christopher Wren suggested a number of ways of accounting for the remarkable event described in the twentieth chapter of the Second Book of Kings. Isaiah the prophet entreated the Lord for a sign to convince King Hezekiah that he would be healed. His request was that the shadow on the King's sundial should go back ten degrees and, according to the ancient narrative, this is what happened. Significantly, at a time when the streets of London were home to all manner of religious fanatics and visionaries, Wren was concerned to propose ways in which this could have happened without outraging the laws of nature.

Wren praised the new freedom in the study and observation of nature and celebrated the work of some of the early Gresham Professors including Gunter and Gellibrand. His tribute to the previous generation of Professors deserves to be quoted *in extenso:*

> Amongst which the useful invention of logarithms as it
> was wholly a British art, so here especially received
> great additions; and likewise the whole doctrine of

magneticks as it was of English birth, by the Professors of this place was augmented by the first invention and observation of the mutation of the magnetical variation; a thing I confess as yet crude, yet may prove of consequence in philosophy and of so great use possibly to the navigator that thereby we may obtain the knowledge of longitudes, than which former industry hath hardly left anything more glorious to be aimed at in art.

In concluding, Wren spoke of London: 'since the professorship I am honoured with, is a benefit I enjoy from this City'. He depicted London as particularly favoured by planetary influences and 'with so general a relish of mathematicks and the liberal philosophia in such measure as is hardly to be found in the academies themselves'. He wishes that the citizens of London should always remain the 'masters of the sea', dwellers in 'an Alexandria, the established residence of the mathematical arts'.

Wren's inaugural lecture was also a kind of manifesto of the new science, and it is discussed in these terms by Michael Hunter in a fascinating essay in his collection, *Science and the Shape of Orthodoxy*. Wren believed that the mathematics of his own day had outstripped ancient authorities, and he proclaimed the new philosophy, based on mathematics and not on the kind of logical demonstrations favoured by Aristotle, as a liberation from the 'tyranny' of Greece and Rome. 'Mathematical demonstrations being built upon the impregnable Foundations of Geometry and Arithmetick are the only truths that can sink into the Mind of Man, void of all Uncertainty; and all other Discourses participate more or less of Truth according as their Subjects are more or less capable of Mathematical Demonstration.'

It is apparent what a radical reappraisal of the sources of traditional authority this 'new philosophy' entailed. According to his friend John Aubrey, Wren was convinced that clarity of thought was more significant than erudition and, although a Dean's son, his attitude to religion was commonsensical and purged of mystery. The historian of the Royal Society, Thomas Sprat, claimed that Wren, like himself, saw in the Church of England, 'the Profession of such a Religion and the Discipline of such a Church which an impartial Philosopher would chuse'.

Wren's lecture breathes a huge excitement at the potential unlocked by the progress in scientific research and the vistas opened up by telescope and microscope. 'Imagine', he says, 'how much the ancient laborious Enquirers would envy us.'

Three years after this seminal lecture, the monarchy was restored and the scientific network which centred on Gresham College played a crucial part in the meetings which led to the formation of the Royal Society. The entry in the first journal book of the Society dated 28 November 1660 reads thus: 'These persons according to the usual custom of most of them met together at Gresham College to hear Mr. Wren's lecture'. Robert Boyle, William Petty and others were there. 'After the lecture was ended, they did according to the usual manner withdraw for mutual converse. Where among other things that were discoursed of, something was offered about the design of founding a college for the promoting of physico-mathematico experimental learning.'

There follows a discussion on the constitution and a great deal of time was spent on this subject. This is understandable in view of the convulsions which London had experienced in the previous twenty years. Gresham College itself had finally become a billet for soldiers in

1659 and many members of the group had raw memories of the effects of social upheaval and religious fanaticism. While the Royal Society took its first steps there was considerable anxiety about the health of its parent body. John Evelyn notes in his diary for 30 July 1662, 'a meeting about charitable uses and particularly to enquire how the City had disposed of the revenues of Gresham College and why the salaries of the Professors there are no better improved. I was on this commission with divers Bishops and Lords of the Council but little was the progress we could make.'

The business of the Royal Society did make progress, however, and a Charter of Incorporation was finally obtained on 15 July 1662. The Royal Society was founded in Gresham College and held most of its early meetings there. Nevertheless, it is true that the two institutions were sufficiently distinct in their aims from the beginning, and from an early date the Royal Society was in search of premises of its own.

Members were dislodged from Gresham after the Great Fire of 1666. The conflagration spared Sir Thomas's great mansion in Bishopsgate and the College was used as a temporary Royal Exchange and for much else. Pepys notes on 7 September 1666: 'This day our merchants first met at Gresham College which by proclamation is to be their exchange.' Room was reserved by the Gresham Committee for the Royal Society, but the overcrowded College was not really suitable for the meetings, which migrated to Arundel House at the invitation of Henry Howard. In 1667 Dr. Wilkins, subsequently Bishop of Chester, proposed that subscriptions should be sought to build a new home for the Society but the members were too poor to sustain the necessary fund-raising effort.

In 1673, a deputation of Gresham Professors and

representatives of the Mercers' Company invited the Royal
Society to return, and the members resolved to do so in
November because of 'the conveniency of making their
experiments in the place where their curator (Robert
Hooke) dwells and the apparatus is at hand' as well as 'of
the hopes they find ground to entertain of meeting with
some considerable benefactions at that end of the city'.
On returning to the College, Royal Society members were
greeted 'with Rhenish wine and mackaroons'. The City
Archives still contain an account of their entertainment.

Hooke's connection with the College antedated the
Fire. In 1664 he was a candidate to succeed Isaac Barrow
as Professor of Geometry, but Arthur Dacres was elected
with the support of the Lord Mayor, Sir Anthony Bateman.
Hooke and his supporters in the Royal Society had
protested. They alleged that the Lord Mayor had no
business to be voting at all on this occasion and that, of
the valid votes cast, Hooke had secured four out of five.
The protest was upheld and Hooke entered upon his long
association with the College.

Ten years later, in the wake of the return of the Royal
Society to premises in the College, the Gresham Committee
gave Hooke £40 to build a turret over his lodgings from
which he could make astronomical observations. This
turret is clearly visible in the print of 1740.

The 1670s, however, were difficult times both for the
College and the Royal Society. Membership declined and
subscriptions were hard to collect. Gresham Committee
minutes also reveal a resurgence of City dissatisfaction
with the way in which the Professors were discharging
their obligations. In November 1673, the committee
ordered that there should be an investigation 'to regulate
the abuses of Gresham College as well by removing
families now residing there and unfit meetings which are

kept there to the disadvantage of the College, as all other that shall be found there'.

The sub-committee charged with looking into these abuses reported in March 1676. They had 'viewed the yard, stables and coach house belonging to this house and upon enquiry found that only two of the readers reside in the house, viz. Dr. Mapletoft, physic reader who keeps in his own hands his lodgings, stable and coach house. Mr. Hooke keeps his lodgings but Mr. Sutton is accommodated with his table. Mr. Jenks, rhetoric reader, accommodates Mr. Sutton with his lodgings.' And so it goes on. Dr. Pope's stable was in the possession of Sir Andrew King, 'who lodgeth in the public rooms of the house'. 'Mr. Meredith and his lodgings are now in the hands of Mr. Crispe who had made great alterations viz hath turned the stable and hay room into a hall and kitchen with a door and steps into Broad Street which the Committee ordered him to shut up and take away because they hold it not fitting that a private passage should be made into a college.'

Ten years later very little had changed, and one of the remedies proposed was that two of the Trustees 'attended by the Clerk shall every day in the next term in the afternoons meet at Gresham College and attend there to hear the said lectures and to take notice if any default be made and who it is that neglects his duty of reading'.

It has to be said however that the response from the London public was not infrequently discouraging. Robert Hooke's diary gives a Professor's view of this period of decline. '12 June 1673 No auditory came morning or afternoon so I read not ... ' 1677 'no lecture but a rusty old fellow walked in the hall from 2 until almost 3 ... ' 1678 'Only one came, peeped into the hall but stayed not.'

Once again, however, if Gresham College was not a success as a teaching institution, it continued to be a significant centre of scientific discussion and research, not least because of the work of Robert Hooke himself.

Born in 1635, he was thirty when elected to the Chair of Geometry. He was one of the two Professors who, according to the survey of 1676, actually resided in the College and he died there in 1703. As the son of a lowly curate on the Isle of Wight, Hooke had none of the financial independence or the useful social connections possessed by so many of the early members of the Royal Society. He frequently suffered from ill health, and contemporary descriptions of him suggest that he was lean, bent and ugly. Pepys mentions him in passing when recording his own admission to the Royal Society: 'Above all Mr. Boyle today was at the meeting and above him Mr. Hooke who is the most and promises the least of any man in the world that ever I saw'.

Hooke was recognised as an outstanding empiric and inventor of scientific instruments. He first met Boyle at Oxford where he constructed for him an air pump, the first made in England. He describes his own meticulous scientific approach in what amounts to a moving credo: 'I neither conclude from one single experiment nor are the experiments I make use of all made upon one subject; nor wrest I any experiment to make it quadrate with any preconceived notion. But on the contrary I endeavour to be conversant in all kinds of experiments and, in all and every one of these trials, I make the standards or touchstones by which I try my former notions'.

In 1662 he was appointed Curator of the Royal Society, charged with furnishing experiments for the fifty or so meetings each year. His appointment as Gresham Professor of Geometry in 1665 gave him the essential financial independence to enable him to continue with his work. That year he also published his great book

Micrographia. The immediately impressive thing about this book is the series of beautifully engraved plates depicting objects of all kinds seen under the microscope. Hooke made the microscope himself. It was the first really efficient compound instrument. The plates of the book continued to be reproduced for the next 200 years.

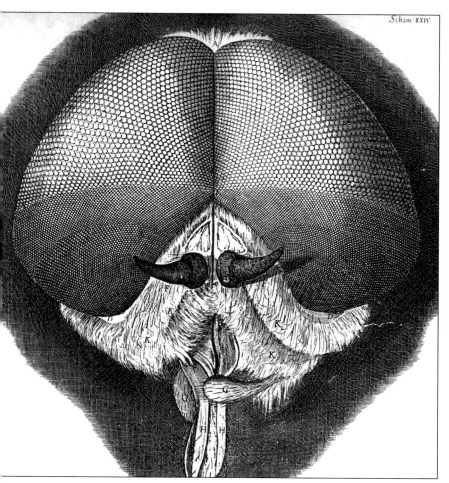

he Eye of a Fly' from Hooke's Micrographia

Micrographia contains a number of fundamental biological discoveries. It describes the life cycle of the gnat. It is in this book that the word 'cell' is first used in its modern biological sense. The whole work teems with fertile suggestions. After discussing threads of natural silk, he writes, 'I have often thought that there might probably be a way found out to make an artificial glutinous composition much resembling if not full as good, nay better, than that excrement, or what ever other substance it be out of which the silk worm wire-draws his clew. If such a composition were found it were certainly an easy matter to find very quick ways of drawing out into small wires for us ... This hint may give I hope some ingenious inquisitive person an occasion of making some trials'.

Pepys records, 'Before I went to bed, I sat up till two o'clock in my chamber reading Mr. Hooke's Microscopical Observation, the most ingenious book that I ever read in my life'. If Newton's *Principia* is a triumph of systematic thought, Hooke's *Micrographia* is a classic of varied and imaginative observations and reflections.

After the Great Fire he assisted his fellow Professor, Christopher Wren, as City Surveyor and he may have been the architect for the building which came to house the Pepys Library at Magdalene College, Cambridge.

His contribution to meteorology was also considerable. He perfected a wheel barometer and a hygrometer. He also invented a wind and rain gauge, but his greatest achievement in the field was the weather clock which recorded, every quarter of an hour, pressure, temperature, rainfall and wind by means of punches operating on a paper strip.

He had theories in the field of geology remarkable for his own time. He regarded fossils as evidence of a past life on an earth which had been formed by great eruptions. Unlike most other contemporary scholars, he never introduced the explanation of Noah's flood to account for the presence of the remains of marine life on high ground.

Some of his non-resident colleagues, however, were also breaking new ground in their very different fields. William Petty was twelve years Hooke's senior. In his youth he had been a pupil and assistant to Hobbes before becoming the Gresham Professor of Music under the Commonwealth. Although he was appointed in 1650, he spent most of his time, not at the College teaching music, but as Physician to the Parliamentary forces in Ireland.

While in Ireland at the end of 1654, he was given the contract to survey all the Irish lands within the space of thirteen months. He registered the data using the services of forty clerks at the Dublin head office and set down the results on maps which were on the scale of 8 inches to the mile. He produced what is still a standard reference work under the title of the Down Survey. It was a masterpiece of practical organisation involving a thousand people who, in Petty's words, had to 'endure travail and also ruffle with the several rude persons in the country'. Petty was paid at the rate of £7 3s. 4d. per thousand Irish acres (1600 English acres), and having discharged all expenses was left with a profit of £9600.

Petty was the founder of a science which has had a very profound effect on modern social and political life. He commended his methods in a book published posthumously in 1690 and entitled *Political Arithmetic,* which was a way 'of reasoning by figures upon things relating to government'. He also published *A Treatise of Taxes and Contributions,* proposed a state medical service and advocated the decimal system.

His was an effort to provide the statistical basis for

transferring the experimental method to matters of public policy. He attempted to get behind the polemics and the bare confrontations of opposing doctrines which had characterised the political debate of the seventeenth century. Although he resigned his Gresham Professorship at the Restoration, he became the Royal Society's expert on trade and industry and thus still a familiar figure at the College.

The Gresham Committee valued the close link with the Royal Society, partly because the alliance seemed a good way to attract an audience to the lectures, 'to answer the intent of the worthy founder which we conceive at present to be wholly defeated and no way serviceable to the public'. It is a lament that has echoed through the past four centuries, in which there has always been a struggle to find the right audience for the lectures even when the College has been successfully operating as an interdisciplinary research institute.

Anxiety about the future of the College came to a head in 1699. The money needed to rebuild the Royal Exchange after the Great Fire had been borrowed at very high interest and the Committee decided that they should attempt to develop the Bishopsgate site. They attempted to procure an Act of Parliament to demolish the old College and erect a smaller one in its place. The plan was to construct other buildings on the site for commercial letting to supplement the waning revenues from the Gresham Estate. The plan was opposed by the Professors who had been making a personal profit by letting their lodgings, in the manner revealed in the enquiry of 1676. The Professors were also concerned at the loss of the facilities enjoyed by the Royal Society and, in particular, the premises of the fine Arundel Library.

The dispute went to arbitration by the Archbishop. The

Bishop of London and the Lord Keeper and the Professors
were won over, all save Hooke who by this time was the
only resident Professor and increasingly infirm. He
submitted a petition against the Gresham Bill when it was
presented in the House of Lords, alleging that the Trustees
had got themselves into a mess by their own
incompetence and by the decision to rebuild the Royal
Exchange on such a grandiose scale. Noble friends of the
Royal Society joined in the attack on the Bill which was
lost when Parliament was dissolved.

After the death of Hooke there was a renewed attempt
to redevelop the site in a way that left no room for the
Royal Society. Isaac Newton drafted a letter to the Queen
petitioning her to grant a piece of land to the Society
because 'the Trustees and Professors of Gresham College
are about pulling down and rebuilding the said College in
a new form which will afford your petitions no convenient
accommodation'. It was not until 1711, however, when
this second scheme had also come to nothing, that the
Royal Society bought the house in Crane Court and the
histories of the College and the Society go their separate
ways after fifty years of cohabitation.

The Gresham College Bill was not finally procured until
1768 and then in a form which destroyed the physical
existence of the College for more than half a century.

GRESHAM COLLEGE IN THE EIGHTEENTH CENTURY

Throughout this period, when the future of Gresham College was so uncertain, the charges of neglect of duty against the Professors continued to rumble on and much energy was expended in pamphleteering and in legal tussles.

There was one such manifestation of public discontent in 1706, possibly fermented by the parish officers of St. Helen's, Bishopsgate, who had been frustrated in their attempts to levy the poor rate on the Professors' apartments individually rather than on the College as a whole. The case came before Sir Thomas Rawlinson, the Lord Mayor, when it was further alleged that the College had lost a legacy of £1900 from a certain Dr. Plume. This gentleman had given the money to Cambridge instead because he saw 'so plainly the abuses of that College'.

The controversy about daily reading of lectures as mentioned in the will was revived, and a group of citizens professedly desirous of self-improvement brought a petition against the lecturers. They claimed that 'when they understood that there were lectures at Gresham College, met in expectation of hearing the same at the usual times they were said to be read, but finding themselves disappointed and nothing performed ... or at least but seldom and in such an indifferent manner when they did, as if the Professors desired to have no company to attend them but be wholly exempt as they formerly had been from taking any pains at all'.

A pamphlet, one of a series preserved in the Guildhall Library and published in 1707, makes the serious point that England was falling behind her European competitors in the provision of university level education. The authors urge that 'few eminent Cities, much less a Metropolis as London, are without their Public Academies, insomuch that there are no less than Twenty in Germany, Twelve in Italy, Sixteen in Spain and its dependent Kingdoms, as many in France, Eight in the Netherlands, Five in Denmark and Poland, Four in Scotland, tho' but Two in England'.

The dispute only ended in 1720 with a resolution broadly in favour of the Professors' understanding of their obligations. Better advertising was instituted, however, and a notice was posted in the Royal Exchange detailing the times and subjects of the lectures.

Nevertheless, useful work was still being done and there is evidence of this in the contemporary account of College activities in John Ward's *Lives of the Professors of Gresham College*. Sometimes the substitutes hired by the Professors to perform their duties were savants of the front rank themselves. The Reverend John Flamsteed is a good example, and it is now possible to read the Gresham Lectures of the future Astronomer Royal, since they were first published in 1975.

Rather late in the day comes an echo of some protest at the submerging of the College beneath the tide of eighteenth century property development. It is contained in a pamphlet, once again preserved in the Guildhall Library, published in Croydon and dated 1784. The title is *Gresham's Ghost - A Tap at the Excise Office*. The whole is presented as a series of complaints addressed to Sir Thomas Gresham in heaven. The 'tap' is delivered in the form of an acrostic, in the first instance upon the text of Jeremiah 7.11: 'Is this house which is called by my name become a den of robbers in your eyes'. When the potential of this phrase is exhausted there follow acrostics formed on the titles of the various Gresham Chairs. The

effect is ingenious rather than profoundly poetical, and the
point is made in the best stanzas and rather blunted by
repetition:

U	Urg'd by a zeal to serve mankind
S	So many ways he strove
E	Each art, each science, every mind
W	Would Gresham fain improve.
H	How must he feel in Heaven surprize
I	If ill he there can know
C	Chang'd when he hears to an Excise
H	His mansion is below.
I	If Naboth's vineyard ill obtained
S	Stands Jezebel's disgrace
C	Can Gresham College be explained
A	A widely differing case?

During its period of near invisibility, the Gresham
committee was preoccupied with questions familiar to
those who remember the homeless period before the
occupation of Barnard's Inn. Once again they were
enquiring in 1799 into 'the management and the
conducting of the Gresham Lectures and how far they are
at present useful and beneficial ... to the public at large
consistent with the intentions of the Founder'.

The enquiry resulted in eight resolutions:
1. To erect a painted board in the Royal Exchange.
2. To provide a finger board pointing the way to the
   lecture room.
3. To station the Keeper with his staff outside the
   doors of the lecture room which were to be open
   an half hour before the beginning of the lecture.
4. To continue the use of both Latin and English.
5. To read the English lecture at noon and the Latin
   lecture at 1pm.

6. To deliver the music lecture at 2pm.
7. To insert a newspaper advertisement at the beginning of term.
8. To require the lecturers to sign the attendance book.

There was yet another enquiry in 1821 and the decision was taken to abandon the Latin lectures. The reason is not hard to seek if one contemplates the attendance figures for the first decades of the nineteenth century which do survive. The average attendance at the English lectures was ten persons per lecture. The average attendance at the Latin lectures was thirteen persons per year. Things were particularly bad during the period of the Napoleonic Wars, and in 1811 the records reveal that there were 301 attendances in all at ninety lectures. It is not necessary to be the Professor of Geometry to conclude that this was a most unsatisfactory state of affairs. As we shall see later, however, it proved not to be possible to suppress the Latin lectures as easily as that.

NINETEENTH CENTURY REFORM
AND THE BUILDING OF THE
SECOND GRESHAM COLLEGE

G hosts may twitter but the College had been invisible for more than half a century when Gresham's legacy came under more purposeful scrutiny in that intoxicating decade of reform, the 1830s. Weighty voices were raised in criticism of what had been done in the Parliamentary Act of 1768.

In April 1836 William Palmer, Gresham Professor of Law, chose to devote his inaugural lecture to the subject of the Gresham Foundation itself. The name of William Palmer will not be unfamiliar to those who are members of the Mercers' Company. This William was cousin to Roundell Palmer, later first Earl of Selborne. He was also son to the Reverend William Jocelyn Palmer, his predecessor as Professor of Law and thus very much one of the family.

In circumspect and orotund terms he put his case. 'I am well aware that in every human institution, whether from defects in its original frame, from the misconduct or honest error of those with whom its conduct rests or from its altered relation with circumstances in the rolling tide of history, there will ever be many faults or imperfections to be found.'

Presumably a Palmer was not in a position to be overly critical of the way in which the previous two or three generations had administered the trust, but, with an insider's authority, the critical observations he made in his lecture caused a great stir. The whole piece was extensively quoted in Dean Burgon's *Life and Times of Sir Thomas Gresham,* which was published in 1839.

The Lord Mayor had offered a prize for the best essay on Sir Thomas Gresham, and Burgon won the competition in 1836 with an essay which grew into his meticulously researched book. Although the author is chiefly known now for his famous lines about Petra, ('rose-red city half as old as time'), a city he had never in fact visited, his book on Gresham played a large part in rekindling interest in the College and its possibilities while inspiring a new generation with the idea that a wrong had been done.

The new Gresham College from the Illustrated London News, *24 June 1843*

The Professor of Music, Edward Taylor, in particular, made his contribution to raising the temperature. He gave his lectures in 1838 in the City of London School, and in a somewhat romantic and histrionic mode he declared that 'Gresham College was levelled to the ground and all trace of its beauty and grandeur obliterated by an Act of the Legislature. I believe that this act of wanton and ruthless barbarism to be without parallel in the history of civilised man ... The present generation hardly knows that there was such a place. Tradition will soon be unable to point out its locality and history alone will inform future ages where once stood its proud and princely halls. All that is now known of Gresham College is the periodical announcement in the newspapers that lectures are to be delivered in the Royal Exchange in an obscure corner and at an inconvenient hour.' Taylor himself broke with tradition in delivering his lectures at 7pm to suit the new hours of City workers.

Mention was also made in Taylor's lecture of the 'late calamitous fire' which razed the second Royal Exchange, the building so expensively restored after the Great Fire. The

agitation proved to be sufficient to ensure that the rebuilding
of the Third Royal Exchange was accompanied by the
construction of a new purpose-built Gresham College at the
cost of £7,000. It was erected at the corner of Gresham
Street and Basinghall Street and opened in 1842.

The second half of the nineteenth century saw an
astonishing increase in the numbers of educational
institutions of all kinds and Gresham College, with its
tradition and central location, might have been thought to
be well placed to take advantage of the new appetite for
learning and its practical applications in the City
environment. There was, for example, a proposal to annex
the Foundation and its revenues to the work being done in
the secondary schools of the City but this was fiercely and
understandably resisted by the Professors.

There seems to have been an incapacity, however, to
seize any new opportunities, and the description of the
experience of attempting to attend a lecture which was
published in the journal founded by Charles Dickens, *All
Year Round,* in 1860 suggests that the College had failed to
find a new niche for itself in the rapidly expanding world of
London education. Since this account is probably from the
pen of Dickens himself it is worth quoting *in extenso:*

> I lighted upon an advertisement in a daily paper setting
> forth that the Gresham lectures for this Easter term would
> be given - certain subjects on certain named days - in the
> theatre of the Gresham College in Basinghall Street, in
> Latin at twelve o'clock and in English at one. I presented
> myself at the Gresham College. A pleasant faced Beadle,
> gorgeous in blue broad cloth and gold, and with the
> beaver-ist hat I had ever seen - a cocked hat bound with
> lace like the Captain's in *Black-Eyed Susan* - was standing
> in the hall and to him I addressed myself, asking where
> the lecture was given. 'In the theatre up-stairs, sir. Come

at one and you'll hear it in English.' 'Isn't it given in
Latin at twelve?' 'Lor' bless you, not unless there's three
people present, and there never is!'

A similar picture emerges from the account by the
journalist Bernard Becker of attending a Geometry lecture
in 1874. According to his essay published in his collection
Scientific London he did succeed in being part of a quorum
of seven that gathered to hear the Dean of Manchester
lecture in Latin on Geometry at 6pm on 23 January. The
Dean did not turn up and a substitute read from a dog-
eared manuscript composed in Latin 'with very little regard
to classic grace, albeit abundantly seasoned with lengthy
Greek quotations, clumsily strung together like pearls on
rotten twine'. Becker's feelings as the evening wore on
alternated between 'calm endurance, nervous irritability,
savage fury and stolid despair'.

He stayed on for Trigonometry in English at 7pm but
was no more edified. Becker concludes that 'it is
disappointing to find that in an age when so much talk is
heard about education, no better employment can be found
for the Gresham bequests than in lectures from which no
human being can possibly learn anything'.

Part of the trouble continued to be that, in the absence
of any other institutional reference point or developed
corporate identity, the scanty indications of the Tudor will
and the few regulations agreed in 1597 provided an excuse
for resisting the kind of change which Sir Thomas himself
would undoubtedly have approved.

In the 1880s there was another attempt to build a
complementary alliance, this time with the City and Guilds
of London Institute which was at first directed from
Gresham College. Philip Magnus in the end preferred
working from South Kensington because 'the Professors of
Gresham College occupy for the great part of the day the

library, which is the only room in which I can work and receive visitors. In the intervals when the professors are not lecturing they frequently sleep at the College using the library as a sitting room and for meals.'

Burgon, in discussing Sir Thomas's intentions in founding the College, used the phrase coined by Sir George Buck and described it as 'the epitome of an university' and one course of development might have been that which was tried in the twentieth century when Gresham was associated with the City University. The idea, however, was already being seriously canvassed at the end of the nineteenth century. In 1892 a Royal Commission investigated the idea of establishing a Gresham University in London.

In the published proceedings, Thomas Boor Crosby MD FRCS, Chairman of the City Side of the Joint Grand Gresham Committee, gave some illuminating answers to the Commissioners which reflect the state of the College at the end of the nineteenth century. He expresses the hope that the name of Gresham might be given to the new university but casts doubt on the extent of practical assistance to the project which could be expected thereafter.

Lord Reay for the Commissioners: Does the Gresham Committee propose to enter the new university as a constituent college? At present you call yourself the Gresham College? - Yes.

Is it proposed that the Gresham College will in the new university have an independent collegiate and corporate existence?

Mr. Crosby: No, because we are not a teaching College. It is a sort of post-graduate course and it is not even a text book teaching College. It has only certain subjects. The will of Sir Thomas Gresham is accurately followed out by paying lecturers to give lectures on certain subjects. There are seven subjects. I have attended these lectures and I think I may say that, for instance, the Geometry lectures would not qualify for any university.

Commissioner: The Lectures then according to you are not all university lectures but some of them are?

Mr. Crosby: They are all on scientific subjects but they are all at the will of the lecturer to please a popular audience ... The lecturer takes from his own subjects what he thinks will amuse. They are not subjects which will pass a test examination for any university.

In such a litigious and controversial history it is easy to understand Mr. Crosby's insistence on following the letter of the Gresham will but, just as Sir Thomas's selection of subjects reflected the needs of the London of his own day, so, if his College is to fulfil his intentions, it has always been necessary for his subject divisions to be creatively interpreted. This has certainly been the pattern in recent years but, in default of this kind of flexibility a hundred years ago, it was modestly proposed that the Gresham College building should be lent as the Senate House for the new University.

In any case there was little room for manoeuvre financially. John Watney, the Clerk to the Gresham Committee, explained the finances to the Commission in greater detail. The income from the estate was £19-20,000 per annum. The seven Professors got £100 apiece exactly as they had in 1768. Another £700 went to the upkeep of the College and the surplus was absorbed by the upkeep of the Royal Exchange itself and not least in servicing the debt.

In the event, the University of London Act of 1898 reconstituted the existing University of London as a teaching university and Gresham College was left out of the new arrangements. By this time, however, the attendance at lectures had revived, as David Vermont explains, and the need for radical reform seemed to be less pressing.

THE FOURTH CENTURY

The three hundredth anniversary of the College gave rise to nothing to compare with the celebrations of a hundred years later. Perhaps that was because there was little to celebrate apart from longevity itself. At this period we find in the Gresham Repertories a bare record of appointments to professorships, of retirements or deaths in office. There is no glimpse of activity nor of the institution's character: few insights, if any, into the intellectual life of the College: no attempt to assess the effect of the lectures. The new statue of Queen Victoria for the Royal Exchange unveiled by the Lord Mayor in 1896 created much more interest for the Joint Grand Gresham Committee, as it was to do again in recent times.

One may assume that the City fathers and the liverymen of the Mercers' Company carried out their duties punctiliously, and indeed there is evidence to show that they did so. These duties, however, did not extend to any close scrutiny of the intellectual impact which the College was having, or not having, on the nation or on the capital. They did, nevertheless, encompass appointments, housekeeping and finance.

Appointments to Professorships from earliest times were the prerogative and responsibility of the two sides of the Grand Gresham Committee, as they still are. In this respect Gresham's executors will have been true to him. There is evidence that great care was taken in making appointments. As in more recent times, expert advice was sought. The Lord Chief Justice, for Law, and the Bishop of London, for Divinity, would on occasion be asked their opinions. Indeed for the Divinity lectureship there were thirty-six candidates in 1904. A short list of six was drawn up, each being required to give a public probationary lecture of half an hour's duration, and members of the Court of Common Council were invited to attend. The Lord Mayor, as Chairman of the Joint Grand Gresham Committee, was asked to fix the date for the election, and he presided over the appointment of the Reverend Dr. W. H. Thompson who won favour with a lecture on 'Nature and Immortality'. It is recorded that the appointment did not carry with it the use of a room, as there is evidence some others did. He continued to give his lectures until the suspension of the College's activities in 1940, and died in February 1945 before the resumption.

The Joint Grand Gresham Committee watched attentively over housekeeping and expenditure. At the turn of the century the College was housed in the building it had occupied since 1842 on the corner of Gresham Street and Basinghall Street. It consisted of a lecture theatre, a library and other facilities. The lecture theatre had seating for 204, plus 180 in the gallery. The gallery was closed in 1908 on the orders of the Fire Officer, and such was the evident popularity of the lectures that the College was enlarged in 1911 when it became possible to acquire an adjacent site. The extension was estimated to cost £20,000 and 24 July 1913 was fixed for the laying of the two foundation stones, still visible today on the building, which is now a bank. The stones were laid by the Master of the Mercers' Company and the Chairman of the City Side: appropriately, in order to demonstrate equality of sponsorship, side by side by the main door in Basinghall Street. The design for the new building was exhibited at the Royal Academy in 1912. Thus the Joint Grand Gresham Committee of the time kept faith with the Founder, referring in January 1911 to 'the great work entrusted to us by the late Sir Thomas Gresham'. And there would thenceforth be accommodation for 420 to 450.

The new building, though costly, was expected to bring in some worthwhile rents from lettings. It must be remembered that in those days the College had no academic staff other than the Professors. It did, however, have a household staff in full-time employment. One member who died in 1931 was the liftman, a Captain A.J. Biddulph OBE, MC and Bar, no doubt a victim of the recession. He was succeeded by another soldier, probably equally worthy, but of lower rank, Sergeant Carroll of the Irish Guards who was paid £3 a week plus £10 per annum for attending evening lectures.

We are told very little of the lecture programme, but interest is kindled in financial matters by such references. Suits were provided at a cost of six guineas in 1936 which went up to £7 10s in 1940.

It is obvious from the keenness with which plans for extending the College were accepted that public lectures in general - and perhaps Gresham lectures in particular - were popular in the early decades of the twentieth century. The requirement was for each Professor to give four lectures a term, there being three terms in a year. The lectures were advertised at the expense of the Grand Gresham Committee and some were printed, although there was a dispute about whether printing was desirable. Some Professors were able to claim additional amounts for costs in illustrating their lectures. Professors' emoluments from 1 January 1921 were set at £150 per annum.

The attendance figures for the Michaelmas Terms in 1926 and 1927 are shown below as probably being not untypical. Total attendance for four lectures is shown, 1926 coming first.

Law: 1142/364; Physic: 950/870; Rhetoric: 716/509; Astronomy: 939/1212; Geometry: 245/322; Music: 1914/1566; Divinity: 744/814.

These can be considered respectable, with Music outstanding. In fact for the Hilary term 1927 the figure of 2000 appears in the minutes with the comment 'hall full every evening'. The Professor of Music since June 1924 was Sir Walford Davies. He succeeded Sir Frederick Bridge, appointed in 1890, who had died in March. Walford Davies was to become Master of the King's Musick on the death of Sir Edward Elgar in 1934. He died in office nearly seventeen years after his appointment.

There is scope for the College one day to publish a book of 'brief lives' of its Professors, for which there will have to be found a latter-day Aubrey. There is one engaging character who shall be mentioned here . He is J. E. Nixon, who resigned his professorship in November 1914 on account of hoarseness, claiming that he had regularly lectured to an audience of 200. He was a Life Fellow and Dean of Trinity College, Cambridge, as well as a lecturer in Latin, and had been Professor of Rhetoric for thirty-eight years. E.F. Benson in *As We Were* (1930) gives a captivating account of a man who:

> for sheer experimentalism ... was farther ahead in the van of progress than the most extravagant of modern pioneers, and had more new notions every day than most people have in a lifetime. He held glee-meetings once a week after Hall, at which he sang Victorian catches and madrigals arranged for male voices. Dr. Ford, the present Dean of York, sat by his elbow, and with him sang the tenor part, while Nixon beat time (like my mother at Lincoln) with a paper-knife. Faster and faster under the intoxication of the music rang out our melodies, until the paper-knife flew from his hand, like Excalibur, and crashed into the fender. Between the songs he handed round hot buttered buns, anchovy toast, Borneo cigars, and Tintara wine.

In person he was small: a short honey-coloured beard framed his chin, he had one glass eye, and only one hand: in place of the other he had a tight black glove (I think pneumatic, for it sometimes seemed to be deflated) which was attached to his wrist, and protruded from the sleeve of his tail-coat. But these physical deficiencies were no handicap to his activity: rather, they seemed to stimulate it, as if he was gallantly bent on showing how much could be done with how little. He rode a tricycle intrepidly about the traffic-crowded streets of Cambridge, he played lawn tennis on fine summer afternoons in the Fellows' Gardens, taking down there a small black bag containing tennis-balls and sealing-wax and pieces of string (for there was no telling whether some emergency would not arise when string or sealing-wax would be urgently required) and Borneo cigars. When he served he lodged a ball in the crook of his arm, and by some unique jerk of his body, tossed it into the air, and gave it a savage underhand blow. Everything he did was performed at top speed, and he generally dropped something. His mind whirled incessantly in a maelstrom of new dodges for counting the attendance of the undergraduates in chapel, for registering votes at Fellows' meetings, for ensuring regular supplies of toilet paper in such places as the dons needed them, or for ascertaining the speed of the train in which he was travelling. He was also (God knows how or why) a Gresham lecturer in London, and I once went up from Cambridge in order to attend one of these discourses. The subject was either 'Poetry in Rhetoric' or 'Rhetoric in Poetry'; but the course of the lecture did not make it clear which it was, and there has been complete confusion in my mind ever since.

Disruption of life in the metropolis was much more severe in World War II than it had been the 1914-18 war. On 1 December 1939 it was announced that the Gresham Lectures would be discontinued till further notice. Elections continued to take place until the death of Sir Walford Davies on 11 March 1941, and at the next meeting of the Joint Grand Gresham Committee it was decided that the post should not be filled and that the other professorships should not be renewed when their terms expired. A subsequent request by the Professors for pensions was turned down.

Use of the College hall was allowed temporarily to the Office of Works and subsequently to the Air Raid Disasters Department. Other users were approved from time to time including one for a police dance. It was recorded in September 1942 that over the previous three months 27,000 people had paid for admission to a series of concerts.

After the end of the war came the resumption of lectures in the Autumn of 1946, after the two sides of the Joint Grand Gresham Committee experienced some difficulty in getting back into their stride. The following appointments were made:

City Side:
Astronomy	Dr William Herbert Steavenson
Divinity	Prebendary Martyn Saunders
Geometry	Professor L.W. Milne Thompson
Music	Peter Latham

Mercers' Side:
Physic	Professor H. Hartridge
Rhetoric	R.W. Jepson
Law	Eric Sachs

R.W. Jepson, whose inaugural lecture the writer remembers attending fifty-one years ago, had just retired as Headmaster of Mercers' School. He resigned from the Professorship after two terms and was replaced by Lord David Cecil, who in turn resigned after four terms on grounds of ill-health and was succeeded by another distinguished English scholar, Nevill Coghill. David Cecil was easily the most popular lecturer, and Nevill Coghill retained the position until overtaken by Eric Sachs in 1950. Average attendances for this period went from about twenty per lecture for Physic to eighty for Music.

1958 saw the transfer of the Gresham Library to the Guildhall Library where it has been looked after ever since. The following is an extract from the Preface to the Catalogue of the Gresham Music Library.

> The library comprised a group of miscellaneous works, mainly travel, and a collection of printed and manuscript music. After the miscellaneous works had been sorted, duplicates and other unwanted material were presented by the Gresham Committee to the Royal Library at Malta and the residue was then incorporated into the general catalogue of Guildhall Library. The music was kept in its entirety and is the subject of this catalogue.
>
> The genesis of the music collection arose from a decision of Edward Taylor, a notable bass singer of the 19th century. Taylor was appointed Gresham Professor of Music in October 1837. He began his duties in January 1838 and on 23rd June he informed the Gresham Committee of the steps he had taken to 'commence the formation of a musical library for Gresham College'.

Other famous people connected with the Gresham Chairs at this time were Thurston Dart (who, acting as a stand-in, paid homage to the first Gresham Professor of Music, Dr John Bull, with a series on Early English Keyboard Music), as well as Stephen Spender and C. Day Lewis.

BABYLONIAN CAPTIVITY

There now appears on the scene a Master of the Mercers' Company, Peter Winkworth, whose energetic enquiries were to have far-reaching effects, not ultimately in a way of which he would have been likely to approve. In 1962 he attended a Gresham lecture and 'raised again the question of the effectiveness and usefulness of the lectures'. He produced a memorandum suggesting an enquiry into the following:

1. How the Lectures could be replanned to serve
   - (a) undergraduates of London University
   - or (b) students at London technical colleges
   - or (c) pupils at London day schools.
2. The subjects of Lectures.
3. The times and frequency of Lectures.
4. Whether the stipends should be revised.
5. What change in publicity was called for.

At last here was somebody prepared to question assumptions which had remained unchallenged for scores of years, if not centuries. He was a lawyer with a broad mind; a scholar with wide sympathies; a man of action whose enthusiam spurred on others. He was also fortunate in having among his Wardens two outstanding men, Lord Ebbisham who was also a member of the Court of Common Council, and Harry Hodson who outranked everyone within sight in terms of academic standing as a former Fellow of All Souls, and who had just retired as Editor of *The Sunday Times*.

Winkworth and the sub-committee he formed were asked to write a report, which in fact saw the light of day only in November 1965 and was presented to the Joint

Grand Gresham Committee on 3 December 1965. The delay was due to the advice he had received to await the Robbins Committee Report on Higher Education which was published in October 1963, but which, as it turned out, had little relevance to the particular position of Gresham College.

The Winkworth report discussed various options open to the College, in particular the possibility of a tie-up with the Sir John Cass Foundation or with the Northampton Polytechnic, and links with the College of the Air and the Royal Society, the latter to revive the early cohabitation.

Things were now moving swiftly and a link with Northampton found favour, partly no doubt because that institution was being transmogrified into City University, with the Lord Mayor as *ex officio* Chancellor. Yet another sub-committee was formed with Dr. Tait, the Northampton Principal, included. This Committee reported on 4 February 1966 that the Gresham Lectures were 'to fulfil the new University's requirement that all engineering and applied science undergraduates should receive fifteen per cent of their formal training in non-technical studies'. On 14 July 1966 Peter Winkworth gave what he called an inaugural lecture, of which 500 copies were printed selling at 3*s*. each, to celebrate this new lease of life for the College; the initial period of the link was for five years. Even those who were to undo, stitch by stitch, the fabric he had started to weave for the College can admire this piece of handicraft by which he tried to provide a decent covering for the exposed parts of that body.

It was undoubtedly an imaginative solution to the problem of what to do with an institution whose existence was being questioned, and whose usefulness was seen to decline as numbers showed renewed signs of falling away. City University, a new and untried university, would have grafted on to it a venerable college which had a name to conjure with, and could provide it with a special connection to the City Corporation and the premier City Livery Company. Gresham College, or at least the Gresham Lectureships, because the College as an entity could hardly be said to exist, would obtain a foster parent who could be expected to understand what it was about, better, perhaps, than its real parents. That the solution had the drawbacks of its own virtues was not seen at the time.

The effect of the link was supposed to ensure for the Professors a captive audience of students and academic staff. The arts subjects would, it was hoped, provide a broadening of the mind in a largely scientific-based curriculum. The appointments, though still nominally under the control of the two sides of the Grand Gresham Committee, would in effect be made by the University. Lectures would be held in the University, but would be open to the general public.

What was not contemplated was that 'it will always be difficult to entice the City worker as far as St John's Street', in the words of a report to the Joint Grand Gresham Committee in 1967. The figures for the second series for 1967 were very low, apart from Anthony Hopkins's Music Lectures and the inaugural Rhetoric Lecture on Copernicus and Galileo by Sir Robert Birley, who had been Headmaster of Charterhouse and Eton and was a great acquisition; he attracted 600. Numbers fluctuated, but there was very little support from the general public, though it was for them that the Lectures were supposed to be given.

Matters came to a head again in 1975 when new proposals were put forward by Lord Alport as Pro-Chancellor of City University and *ex officio* Chairman of the University Council. These constituted an extension of the 1966 basis of co-operation, and sought to provide for the future of Gresham College as an integral part of City University. Gresham College would therefore lose its separate identity, if it had not lost it already, but would itself absorb the following functions of the university:

- The Graduate Business Centre (later to become the City University Business School)
- The International Banking and Finance Unit
- The Arts Administration Course
- The Music Degree Course
- The General Studies and Extra-Mural Department of City University.

It would also provide the Gresham Lectureships. There was much else about fellowships, finance, governance and academic development.

In the next three years very little happened. In 1979 it was reported that the Vice-Chancellor had found it necessary to defer implementation of the 1976 proposals which had been agreed, mainly because of constitutional reasons deriving from the University's charter[1]. So yet another scheme was put forward, which still sought to provide for the incorporation of the College within the University. We read that D. Silk (City) and J.D. Watney (Mercers'), both lawyers, wished to vary the scheme, but were outvoted: the first rumblings perhaps of objection to what was otherwise an automatic rubber-stamping machine.

On 18 April 1980 the Joint Grand Gresham Committee

1. See Memo of Vice-Chancellor dated 20 June 1979 reported to JGGC 6 July 1980. The proposals, it was said, produced conflicts of interest and would need statutory authority before implementation. In any case, departmental mergers no longer appeared suitable: for instance the Graduate Business Centre had become the City University Business School.

again considered proposals for the establishment of a Council of Gresham College and a Gresham College Trust through which the necessary finance would be made available to the College. It was becoming apparent that the College had no corporate existence, a deficiency which Council would ultimately seek to remedy in a more conclusive way.

These proposals, the product of a working party, are contained in the Clerk's[2] Memorandum dated 18 April 1980, and dealt in a comprehensive fashion with the purpose of the College, its governance and relationship with its now three sponsoring bodies, as well as with finance. The Company and the Corporation always took fright at any new proposal which might involve further subventions, and we read the chilling passage: 'It was clearly understood that there was no financial commitment on the part of the Mercers' Company or the Corporation and it would be for them to decide whether, and if so, to what extent, they would contribute to the Trust'. On the other hand one provision was forward-looking, giving the Trustees power to accept donations 'from any source, such as industry, commerce, the University, The Mercers' Company, and other Livery Companies, the Corporation and the City and business institutions'.

The recommendations of the working party were adopted, and appointments were made by the two sides. City University accepted the recommendations with alacrity and the Vice-Chancellor, Raoul Franklin, set about not only nominating four university representatives to the

2. The Clerk, so described subsequently, was, and is, Michael Wakeford, from 1974 Clerk (Chief Executive) to the Mercers' Company and Clerk to the Joint Grand Gresham Committee. A man of considerable intellect and great influence in the City, he was a member of the College Council from the start, brooding silently over meetings and acting as a prophylactic against aberration and malevolent intent.

Council to join three Mercers and three Common Councilmen, but also providing lists of Visiting Professors and Research Fellows. Lord Ebbisham was appointed Chairman, the Lord Mayor taking the largely honorary position of President; and David Jenkins, Head of the Centre for Arts and Related Studies in the University, was made Dean for a period of three years.

Moving the Gresham Lectures to Islington made the College building on the corner of Gresham Street and Basinghall Street redundant. Letting it substantially added to the incomes of the Company and the Corporation. A sub-committee of the Joint Grand Gresham Committee reporting on 5 July 1983 came to the conclusion that a permanent home should be found for the lectures in the City and quoted the obligation imposed by the Act of Parliament of 1767[3] at the time of the sale of Gresham's Mansion in Bishopsgate. The proposal, which seemed a good idea at the time, was for the College to take a lease of part of Level 12 of Frobisher Crescent in the Barbican. Besides the return to the City, the move would bring the College alongside the Business School. So the College took on half a floor, the equivalent of 8500 sq. ft., with funding being provided by Company, Corporation and University. It was not appreciated at the time that

---

3. Gresham's Mansion was sold to the Crown for the purpose of erecting a new Excise Office. The Act stipulated as follows: 'And be it further enacted by the authority aforesaid, that the Mayor and Commonalty and Citizens of the City of London, and the Wardens and Commonalty of the Mystery of Mercers of the City of London do and shall, from time to time and at all times hereafter, find and provide sufficient and proper place or places for the present Seven Professors, and all succeeding persons to be chosen, nominated, and appointed for the reading the Lectures in Divinity, Astronomy, Musick, Geometry, Law, Physick, and Rhetorick, to read the same in accordingly; and also like sufficient and proper place and places for the habitation of the Eight Alms-Folks now or hereafter for the time being'. There can be little doubt that the intention was to provide a new replacement building and the Basinghall Street building is evidence of this interpretation.

Frobisher Crescent represented little advance on Islington as regards accessibility, and meant an outlay which was hardly justified even by the supposed benefits of location. The Barbican is an inhospitable place at the best of times, and times were not good. But at least the sponsors were acknowledging their financial responsibility.

Soon after, matters began to get out of hand. The Clerk's Memoranda show some impatience, not a defect which usually afflicted him, at least when he was on record. There was delay in the appointment of Professors, Council having failed to make recommendations. Then a Memorandum of 8 October 1984 disclosed the proposals of the Dean, David Jenkins: a programme of seminars, conferences and short courses for which fees would be charged and which were bound to alter the nature of the College. It was also intended to appoint three additional Professors in Management, Ethics and Education. The Clerk, reiterating growing criticism, wrote: 'Concern has been expressed already at the effect of the proliferation of Gresham Professorships and also at the appointment of "in house" academic staff, however distinguished'. The Professors proposed were all from the University, the Dean himself being among them. Jenkins then submitted a long justification for his plans, which some regarded as ill-advised, and pointing in the wrong direction; but nevertheless the plans were endorsed by Council on 22 October 1984. The positive view prevailed, but not without another thunderbolt from the Clerk who wrote in a Memorandum which fairly presented both sides of the argument: 'The Dean's proposals do not have the hallmark of a carefully thought through scheme. In fact the impression is given of a proposal hurriedly put together based on individuals rather than an objectively defined policy'.

The first meeting of the expanded Professorial body took place on 23 April 1985, attended by ten Professors, the Professor of Music being absent. It will readily be calculated that another Professor had crept in. He was in fact the Gresham Professor of Commerce, about whose appointment there was no dissent. His Chair was sponsored in 1984 by the Mercers' School Memorial Trust, and appointments were made thenceforth by the Mercers' Company after consultation with the Trustees and the College Council.

There must now be some consideration of the attitudes of those who were taking sides in what was becoming a dispute which was rapidly showing signs of being insoluble without drastic measures. The University Officers, led by the Vice-Chancellor, had been unfailingly courteous and helpful, and had moreover shouldered their share of the increasing financial burden. They saw a good opportunity to forge a link with an ancient institution which could add by absorption to the University's prestige. Some academic members, led by the Dean who was given an extension of his appointment in May 1984, were naturally excited by the prospect of professorships. There was also a proposal for a profit-sharing scheme. The University representation on the Council was completed by the co-option of Lord Alport, whose sympathies were absolutely with absorption.

The attitude of the City Side and of the Court of Common Council as a whole cannot be so easily described. Wilfrid Dewhirst became Deputy Chairman of Council in May 1983, and he worked assiduously thereafter, particularly on succeeding to the Chairmanship in October 1985, to keep the show on the road, using his not inconsiderable diplomatic and administrative skills. Peter Revell-Smith and John Holland, the other City Side members of Council, were finding that they were increasingly unable to justify the College's pretensions to a sceptical and generally hostile Court, which had ultimate financial control of the City Side's contribution. When one day soon the Court of Common Council's moral obligation was invoked, this period would be remembered. The frustration this produced was compounded by a healthy mistrust of academics, and with a less healthy admixture of philistinism.

The Mercers, being of a similar breed, showed matching reactions. Lord Ebbisham, whose considerable powers were failing towards the end of his life, was unable to give a lead. The responsibility, therefore, rested on Harry Hodson and David Vermont, who had been members of the Council from the outset. They were enthusiastic about the future of the College, but were adamant that it had taken the wrong path. There was little enthusiasm elsewhere in the Company. Indeed, the Master at that time said later that his eyes glazed over when he heard the name 'Gresham'. The Clerk, when it was pointed out to him that the bidding prayer at the Mercers' quarterly Court Chapel Service required those present to pray for Gresham College at the top of a list of educational establishments supported by the Company, said that his lips never moved.

When Dewhirst succeeded Lord Ebbisham in October 1985 Vermont was offered the Vice-Chairmanship. He declined it, although he was next in line, so that he would be better able to seek to reverse a policy which he and Hodson, as well as Holland and Revell-Smith, thought was ruining the College. All these could count on the support of Alderman A.M. Graham, a Mercer representative who was later to become Lord Mayor of London.

There were many signs of strain. The Professors were

becoming disaffected. The short-course programmes were not developing as anticipated. There was talk of a rescue operation. The Dean admitted there was difficulty in reaching financial targets. The objectives of the College were questioned. A passage from the Council minutes dated 21 January 1986 reads:

> It was generally recognised that after some 18 months' operation, Gresham College was clearly failing to achieve the academic objectives and financial targets set for it during the ten-year period leading to its re-establishment in 1984.

> The links with the City University through its Business School and Department of Arts Policy & Management had not developed on the lines intended, and the absence of any clear distinction between the respective functions of the College and those departments of the University with which it was to have been particularly closely associated had led to confusion and conflict of interest. There was nevertheless support on all sides for improving relationships between the College and the University but the prior need was to clarify the objectives of the College and the roles and status of the Gresham Professors.

At that meeting there was the first mention of a 'minimalist' approach which would involve a drastic reorganisation of the College and the professorships. A month later Hodson, in responding to Lord Alport's defence of his Advisory Committee's opposition to retrenchment, emphasised that the 'minimalist' approach was not intended to be a solution in itself to the College's present difficulites, but rather a base from which to make a fresh start.

A Special Meeting at the University was called for 17 March 1986 at which there was a long and, at times, heated discussion. Vermont moved as follows:

1. That the limitation in prospective income requires substantial and early reduction in expenditure.

2. That, accordingly, it be agreed in principle that, *with effect from the end of the current academic year:*

    (a)   the basic activities of the College be concentrated on those associated with the seven ancient Gresham Professorships;

    (b)   a new relationship with City University be explored with a view to the present Terms of Association being abrogated.

3. That it be referred to the Finance & General Purposes Committee to consider in detail the implications and possible consequences of these decisions.

The motion was carried by four to two with four absentions. Lord Alport resigned immediately and left the meeting. At the next meeting on 1 May the post of Dean was abolished as from 31 July, and Jenkins was given leave of absence till then. Dewhirst, Holland and Vermont were appointed to yet another sub-committee, this time with power to act as the executive body of the College, and with direct access to the Joint Grand Gresham Committee until a new Council was constituted. The sub-committee, subsequently augmented by Hodson[4], met eleven times in the next year. On 23 April 1987 the Council met, Dewhirst being elected Chairman and Vermont Deputy-Chairman, and received a report from the sub-committee redefining academic aims and providing for

---

4. The four members were, of course, members of the JGGC for most of the time. By this time Vermont had also become a member of the Council of City University.

a restructuring of the constitution of the College Council. To show continuing goodwill towards the University, the Vice-Chancellor was to be a permanent member of the Council, which he is to this day.

THE PROMISED LAND

Council now set about the task of improving the image of the College and recasting its finances. The new professorships were eventually disbanded, although the Chair of Commerce was reconfirmed with a new incumbent, the Reverend Jack Mahoney, an eminent Jesuit scholar. Frobisher Crescent was given up as part of the process of retrenchment and the College operated from Mercers' Hall. David Bryden was recruited as Academic Administrator, but he resigned after a year and was replaced by Howard Truelove, who was appointed to the permanent post of Educational Assistant of the Mercers' Company, to run concurrently. Brian Collyer, having originally been seconded by the Company, of which he was Assistant Clerk at the end of his long career, retired from being Clerk to the Council and Bursar, and his functions were taken over by Howard Truelove and Guy Neely, who was Treasurer of the Company. Dewhirst lost his place on Common Council at the elections in December 1987, and Vermont took over the Chairmanship of Council. Proposals were made for Chairs to be advertised in future, and emoluments were revised to a more realistic figure of £3000 per annum. Vermont proposed that Professor Peter Nailor should act in the capacity of Academic Advisor, and he attended his first meeting in January 1988. Wakeford gave a hint that the Mercers' Company would gain vacant possession of Barnard's Inn, which for the first sixty years of the century had been the home of Mercers' School; and thereafter a move to that location became the devout wish of the Council.

The following held Chairs at the end of 1988[5]:

Divinity	The Reverend Richard Chartres
Music	Peter Renshaw
Astronomy	Raymond Hide FRS
Law	Kenneth Simmonds
Rhetoric	John Rae
Physic	Sir Kenneth Stuart
Geometry	Christopher Zeeman FRS
Commerce	The Reverend Jack Mahoney SJ

These were all highly regarded men, who served the College well and responded enthusiastically to the new opportunities provided by a more stable regime.

A new academic leader of a similar standing was obviously necessary, albeit on a part-time basis. Council had some fun choosing a title, Oxford with a kaleidoscope of names for heads of houses being a better hunting-ground than Cambridge. 'Dean' had lost its flavour; 'Master' was too pretentious, as was 'President'; 'Warden' might have been confused with the Livery; 'Rector' smacked too much of the Church; 'Principal' was not pretentious enough; so 'Provost' was chosen, more in the end by process of elimination, although a strong reason was that Hodson had not long since retired from being Provost of Ditchley. Peter Nailor, shortly to retire as Professor of History and International Affairs at the Royal Naval College, Greenwich, was offered the post and accepted with alacrity.

---

5. The scope of the three science chairs was soon after defined as follows:
   Astronomy, and all the physical sciences
   Physic, and all the biological sciences
   Geometry, and all the mathematical sciences
These descriptions certainly became necessary with Lord Porter's appointment as Professor of Astronomy, as he had been awarded the Nobel Prize for Chemistry.

The conjunction of Nailor and Vermont was both felicitous and fruitful. They were old friends, having been at Mercers' School together in the 1940s. They were both liverymen of the Company. The prospect of returning to

Barnard's Inn, home of the School till its closure in 1959, excited both men. There indeed was the promised land.

Meanwhile, there was work to do, to convince both the Corporation and the Company that the College was about to experience a renaissance. There was a major debate in the Court of Common Council in April 1989, when the backwoodsmen came out in an attempt to deprive the College of the necessary funds for its plans. John Holland stood manfully, like Horatius at the bridge.

Barnard's Inn, from a drawing by B.C. Boulter

It was accepted by both Company and Corporation that the Professors' stipends were a first charge on the Gresham Estate, although there was some reluctance to see them set at the standard higher level of £2000 per annum (£3000 from July 1990, £3750 from September 1995). What had to be fought for was the acceptance that there was a moral responsibility to provide funds for housing the College and paying for its administration. The College had always had a home until it was absorbed by the University, and now was the time for it to have a home again. There is a certain irony in the effect which a tax case, lost by the Corporation in the Court of Appeal in 1897, has had on attitudes. The Corporation was required to pay tax on the income from the Royal Exchange shops, it being found that such income was the Corporation's absolutely and not held in trust. The Company was mentioned in the case, as being in a similar position as regards its moiety. The rent from the former College premises in Basinghall Street has been treated in the same way, although the Court of Appeal Judgment emphasises that some parts of the Gresham Estate were subject to trusts. This matter remains to be resolved, although with more generous grants forthcoming, the crisis subsided[6].

The Company was mellowing, worn down by the enthusiastic advocacy of Vermont; and a succession of Masters among whom may be mentioned Lord Selborne, Adrian Watney and John Fenwick, lent powerful but not uncritical support. Revell-Smith relinquished the Deputy Chairmanship in July 1991 and was replaced by Brian Wilson, but remained on the Council as a powerful force for good. At the same time the College advertised for an Academic Administrator. There were over one hundred applicants and Maggie Butcher was appointed. From the start she bade fair to accomplish much, and the success of the College since the move to Barnard's Inn is due in no small measure to her enterprise, enthusiasm and painstaking administration.

It was obvious that the College would be judged both

---

6. The dispute concerned the interpretation of the Customs and Inland Revenue Act 1885 (Section 11). The Divisional Court in finding that the Corporation, in respect of its moiety, was not liable to pay tax on the surplus rents from the Royal Exchange shops refused the plea of the Commissioners of Inland Revenue who contended that the surplus rents belonged to the Corporation for their own benefit absolutely. On 12 April 1897 Chitty LJ, sitting in the Court of Appeal with the Master of the Rolls and Lopes LJ who both concurred, found against the Corporation and so the judgment of the lower court was reversed. It is interesting to note that the case involved only the rents from the Royal Exchange shops. At the time expenditure considerably exceeded income. By losing the case the Corporation (and the Company) ultimately benefitted to the detriment of the College.

by its output and by those associated with it. There was a constant turnover of Professors as the Council instituted a policy of recommending appointments for three years, except for Rhetoric which was for two years. Among those who were invited to become Professors were Lord Porter, Nobel Prize Laureate and former President of the Royal Society (Astronomy); Sir Andrew Derbyshire, a distinguished architect and town planner (Rhetoric); Sir David Calcutt QC, Master of Magdalene College, Cambridge (Law); and Sir Christopher Zeeman, Vice-President of the Royal Society and Principal of Hertford College, Oxford (Geometry); but very soon the appointments were made solely on the basis of interview subsequent to advertisement.

Council, consisting of Corporation and Company appointments as well as representative Professors, used its powers to co-opt wisely, and recruited, among others, Sir Anthony Kenny, former Master of Balliol, Sir Brian Corby, Chairman of Prudential, and George Webb, a former diplomat who in October 1992 took over the clerkship from Howard Truelove. He held the position for two years. Both Truelove and Webb remained members of the Academic Board and Webb stayed on as a member of Council, continuing to be fully involved with the College in these capacities as well as in the arrangement of additional lectures.

The College took up residence in the Gatehouse of Barnard's Inn in the second half of 1991 as tenants of the Company. This gave adequate accommodation for administrative functions, the arrangements providing for the College to have priority use of the Hall for lectures and meetings. In its new home attendances increased. It was seldom that the hundred mark was exceeded but Sir Christopher Zeeman could easily attract over 250 youngsters to his mathematics lectures, which had to be held elsewhere.

Before Vermont retired at the end of 1992 after five years as Chairman, he set in train a further reform of the constitution and on 8 December 1994 Gresham College for the first time became a legal entity, having assumed the status of a Company Limited by Guarantee. The purpose of this move was 'to allow it to breathe its own air' and to wean it from its sponsors. Future generations will see what it makes of this opportunity.

Vermont's successor was Brian Wilson. He provided a safe pair of hands and, as a former Chief Commoner, carried considerable weight with the City fathers. He is a no-nonsense Yorkshireman, and the Corporation soon saw that support for the College was to be the rule. That it had earned such support there could be no longer any question. The distinction of the Professors, and their commitment to collegiality; the effectiveness of the partnership of Provost and Academic Administrator[7], and their co-operation with a fully committed Chairman and Council; a burgeoning academic programme; visibility ensured by a permanent home: all these factors conspired to produce success. But the measurement of success is not easy. Lord Selborne, in his time as Master, had been very keen on peer review, but the difficulty was that the College does not fit into any category. Nevertheless the policy of *reculer pour mieux sauter*, which has won the day, was seen to have been justified.

There is no space in this brief history for a discussion of the academic programme offered in the 1990s, but some aspects need comment. Not only have there been

---

7. Maggie Butcher's title was changed in 1996 to that of Academic Registrar to acknowledge the increasing responsibilities of the post and her success in filling it.

lectures as prescribed, (it must be said that the norm and indeed the requirement has become three lectures in each of two semesters); but often conferences and seminars were arranged; books were commissioned; and each year a Special Lecture has been given to a large audience on an important subject[8].

Council continues to be concerned about attendances. Some subjects attract few people while others, such as Geometry, can count on hundreds. Peter Hennessy (Rhetoric), on British Prime Ministers, had admiring crowds at Barnard's Inn, many sitting on the floor. A series initiated by the Provost and Academic Registrar and implemented with the assistance of Tim Connell of City University and George Webb which was entitled 'Mondays at One', has a substantial following, and provides lectures on a variety of subjects beyond the set curriculum.

All lectures are now printed, and demand for copies is substantial and increasing all the time, a tendency which can be ascribed both to the quality of what is on offer and to the renown of the institution and of its Professors. The process forms a 'virtuous circle' with potentially no limit. That is why it is important that the College must not feel hemmed in by the restrictions which its current sponsorship places upon it.

The four-hundredth anniversary provides a suitable time for consideration of the long-term future. Its stated aim is still to reinterpret the 'new learning of Sir Thomas's day in contemporary terms', but if Gresham College has one virtue above all others, it is its neutral status. It is not beholden to the State for funds, and accordingly is under

---

8. See Appendix for list of Special Lectures. That of Ralph Dahrendorf in May 1989 had an even wider circulation and was evidently avidly read in Eastern Europe by those who were about to rid themselves of their communist shackles.

no pressure to do its bidding. A succession of Gresham Professors has testified to the great value they attach to this position. It was accurately and felicitously described by Richard Chartres as 'benevolent neutrality'[9]. In that, the College has few equals.

Peter Nailor who, as the first Provost under the new dispensation, contributed so much to the achievement of the College's present standing, died in 1996 and was succeeded by Dr Andreas Prindl, an American banker resident in England who had already served on the College Council. The Chairman of the Council in this four-hundredth anniversary year is Francis Baden-Powell, who was Master of the Mercers' Company when it celebrated its six-hundredth anniversary in 1994.

---

9. 'Venture Intellectualism', another memorable phrase, was thought up by Guy Neely, through which he sought to project the College while capturing the spirit of the age. After a career in industry he became Treasurer of the Mercers' Company and subsequently of the College as well as Secretary of the new board.

APPENDIX I

Inaugurating Lecture at Barnard's Inn Hall
by Professor Peter Nailor MA
Provost of Gresham College
15 October 1991

NEW CHALLENGES FOR
THE NEW CENTURY

This is the first occasion for many years on which this
Hall has been used for educational purposes, and I
want therefore to begin by welcoming you to Gresham
College's new home. This beautiful room and an even
more comfortable seminar room downstairs will provide
the location at which most, if not quite all, of our activities
will now take place. Only when there is an audience to
be numbered beyond our capacity here, or when there are
special presentational requirements, shall we stray further
afield than these Western fringes of the City.

But, though it is a new home for the College, for some
of us it is an old homecoming. This Hall was an integral
part of Mercers' School from 1894 until 1959 and I, like the
Chairman of the Gresham College Council, and several
others of you here this evening, know it principally as the
dining hall of our school days, although from 1946
onwards it was used for other purposes as well. It is
therefore a particular pleasure for me to be able to launch
it upon its new course – and to test its hammer-beamed
acoustic. Imagine, if you can, what it was like crammed
with long tables and benches, and the clatter of knives

and forks, and noisy boys. The offices we now have used to be the porter's lodge and the Masters' Common Room, so they too are redolent of past times: and the charming reception room across the lobby here used to be the Headmaster's Study. Even now, after all these years, I cannot go into it without a familiar and guilty feeling that I have not done my Latin prep.

What I want to do in this initial lecture is to sketch out some of the challenges which we here in Gresham College and you here in the City of London will be trying to deal with over the forthcoming years. The Gresham Lectures began, when the College was first established, in 1597: and so, although we have not quite reached our four-hundredth anniversary, we are now so close to it, and our new home here is so significant a gain for us, that a new century is opening up very quickly before us, and we have a new prospect – perhaps a millenary prospect if we are successful – to contemplate.

The broader prospect is equally challenging. Whatever '1992' will eventually amount to for the states of the European Community, we are all on the threshold of new developments that will certainly impinge upon our lives, our institutions and our prosperity. The reverberations that the collapse of the Socialist Second World will cause for us here in the advanced economies of the First World can still only be dimly discerned. What they will mean for the citizens of what has so casually been called the Third World can as yet only be imagined. There will be, at the very least, a lot of hard thinking to do, and a lot of what politicians delicately call 'difficult decisions' to face.

Let me start at the strictly domestic end of this spectrum. What we do in Gresham College is largely defined for us by our historical setting. The way in which Gresham College was established to bring 'the new learning' to the City of London was conceived in a structure of established academic disciplines; lectures were to be given in Divinity, Rhetoric, Astronomy, Music, Law, Physic and Geometry. To these we have added recently the Mercers' School Memorial Chair of Commerce, as an eighth Gresham Professorship. We have also, over the years, construed the classical disciplines in ways that reflect how knowledge has expanded. So, Astronomy is now regarded as representing all the physical sciences, and Rhetoric offers so broad a compass that it can be used to provide an opportunity to engage a range of distinguished exponents of disciplines which in the sixteenth century had not yet cohered: education, for example, and, in the person of the current holder of the Chair, Sir Andrew Derbyshire, architecture. The other founding disciplines have grown so prodigiously that it is possible to use them too in ways that reflect the diversity, not only of knowledge itself, but of the fringes of knowledge represented by research, on the one hand, and public interest, on the other.

We are able, as a consequence, to present a regular programme of lectures and seminars which, within the specialist skills and expertise of our Professors, provide informative expositions about current issues of interest and recent developments, arising from their own research. By their very nature, they tend to be topics which stand at some distance from the day-to-day preoccupations of the general audiences which hear the lectures: but which also, increasingly, avail themselves of the transcripts or summaries which we prepare for a wider distribution. It is often in this way that specialist interest in the lectures is most obviously shown. I ought here, I think, to make a point that we sometimes wonder what we might do to ensure larger audiences than we occasionally get. It is a topic that has surfaced many times in the College's history, and I make no apology for raising it again. For it is a conundrum to which there is no simple solution: and it worried our predecessors, for example, at the same time, in the 1660s, as the evening seminars of the Society of Virtuosi attracted men like Pepys and Evelyn, and Christopher Wren, and gave rise to the Royal Society. Lectures are like other forms of good intelligence; what we have to take account of is not only the substance of the material itself in the form in which it is delivered but the ways in which it is disseminated. If I may adapt Francis Bacon's great adage about prosperity, lecture material and money are both like muck, 'not good except they be spread'. It is always unlikely that an initial exposition will attract a representative audience for which the material has an interest. This is no less true of lectures than research analyses, or sermons or, alas, political speeches; and no good intelligence is of any value unless it is spread, to reach the people who can use it and who need to know about it.

If you consider the community to which Gresham College is particularly committed to serve, the City of London, it has always been difficult to conceive that many in such a diverse and busy community would be physically able to attend set-piece occasions, even if they were aware that they were to be held. If that problem was in any way valid in Stuart or Hanoverian London, it is much more likely to be a factor today, in a London in which not many of its workers live, and in which Greenwich Mean Time is only one of many ways of calculating when the pressure of business demands attention. What is New York time, or Frankfurt, or Tokyo, time is at least as significant to many people in the Square Mile, not to mention the pressures exerted by the latest rumours about whether Fenchurch Street or Cannon Street are operating smoothly, or whether the Drain to Waterloo has gone down the tube again.

The pressures of modern life inform against Gresham College as they do against everyone else, and present us with a challenge – not a new one, as I have indicated, but one to which we must try and find new ways to respond. Better mailing lists and publicity: perhaps. But, at the moment at any rate, I am inclined to think that better, quicker, more extensive dissemination might be a more serviceable way to spread the words we have. We must find a way that does not add to the pressures that our potential audiences already have, but which enables them to assimilate what we have to say, when they can.

This leaves on the one side, of course, the issue of quality: the value and interest of what we do in the first place. That has, primarily, to be judged upon its own merits. But let me note here that the sponsors of Gresham College have paid a lot of attention to ensuring that the appointments to the College embody real distinction, and challenging scholarship.

In addition, they have encouraged the College to move beyond the traditional lecture programme which, with the best will in the world, is defined in the historically constrained way that I have described. We are able now, in a modest but fruitful way, to add a new range of activities to our programme. We are able to support research initiatives by the Professors, which enable them to extend the role they can play, and we can initiate other studies and debates about matters in which the City has a proper concern. So, we can provide a window, by which the City may avail itself of the opportunity to find out what is happening in the world of scholarship; and we can also provide a window through which the City can make known its own interests and concerns. There is an additional factor, too. The particular circumstances of Gresham College itself enable us to offer a form of activity which has a unique independence: we can offer a 'benevolent neutrality' and a very wide interest in holding contemporary problems up to the light. The College programme, of which copies are available here this evening, provides the details of what we are up to, both in our historic pattern and in our newer range of activity. Think of it, if you will, as a range of intellectual investments, with a narrower and a wider band, like trustees and charities can have.

So, if I may take some selective examples from our current work, we are supporting the production of video tapes for use in schools and colleges, about mathematical topics and problems, which provide expert and specialist demonstrations of mathematical principles. These support a general objective of enhancing the standards of mathematical teaching. We have provided assistance for the development of performance and communications skills at the Guildhall School of Music, which enhance that excellent institution's own programme, and have significant applications for the effectiveness of all conservatoires. It is, if you like to draw out its longer-term purpose, a contribution towards ensuring that the very high standards in the Performing Arts (of which our sponsors, in their other functions, are such important patrons) are maintained in all their vivacity for the future, but are also developed. We provide help for the new journal on Business Ethics, which will consolidate the pioneering work in this field which the Mercers' School Memorial Professor of Commerce has so effectively achieved. We are assisting the Gresham Professor of Divinity in his work in the Citizenship Project, which is taking forward the conclusions of the Report on Citizenship that was sponsored by the Speaker of the House of Commons last year. This project will focus attention, and stimulate action, on the duties, as well as the rights and responsibilities, that citizenship and involvement in civic society entail. Nobody could doubt the importance, or the need, for these subjects to be given the best of attention.

More widely, we have recently organised successful conferences and seminars on the relationships between the countries of the Community and the new Europe, on the control of multinational corporations, on the range of ways in which provisions for education in the 16-19 year old range can be developed, and on the challenges to medical education which recent advances in medical and scientific research present. We also support a programme of seminars for the trustees of charitable organisations, who often lack guidance and information about what their responsibilities entail. We have helped with a series of instructional seminars that show senior management personnel what the capabilities of new information technology are. So often senior personnel get by-passed in the acquisition of new techniques and skills, and they need an opportunity to catch up – before they are caught out, pretending to be as jargon-laden and machine-dependent as their junior colleagues.

Finally let me mention two other examples of our activity. First, the College is about to receive a stock-taking report that will lay out the current difficulties and future prospects of the main elements in the voluntary sector. We hope that this will focus attention, and offer some guidance, in an area that is very large, very complicated and really rather important. We have also just begun, and still in a rather tentative way, to enquire into a series of predicaments that the Professor of Rhetoric has suggested we call 'The Culture of Cities'. It is fairly easy to list the main advantages – and the main problems – that people who live in large conurbations experience. But there are many less evident and less straightforward factors which contribute towards a sense of community and of fulfilment – or which detract from it. There are considerations too about what is likely in the future to change or influence the lot of city-dwellers; shall we all work from home, and shop from a TV console? Will the electric car ever happen? And, even if we find who wants to live in the Inner City, can we find anyone who wants to teach, or keep a shop, or sweep the street there? What is it that will make them feel they sufficiently belong to the place to want to stay, to want to contribute to the order, the peace and the beauty of the place? This, I think, will keep us going for a bit; and if the description I have given sounds unfocussed as well as ambitious, I have to say that most of the other thoughts and enquiries we know about that relate to the environment of cities, are much more narrowly-focussed. We want to look at some of the issues that may fall between the cracks: and I'm encouraged that some of the comments in a recent report from the London Chamber of Commerce about the attractiveness of London as a place to live and work for foreign businessmen touched upon some of the broader concerns that we want to think about.

All of this, I think, shows not only a diversity in our activities, but a liveliness and an awareness of current issues which buttress our traditional concerns. It is a solid programme, and of course it is limited in size and scope. But it offers a model for what we want to go on to do, and it illustrates what can be done, with a small office, with a small but distinguished group of scholars who come to Gresham College from their other posts and activities when they can, and with supportive, but by no means complacent, Trustees. We are, in truth, a small and rather odd institution: a 'one-off' model which shares with only one or two other academic corporations in the Western World that enormously privileged position of having many friends, and no students.

If you were to ask me 'what comes next?' for Gresham College, I think I should want to split my answer into three parts. In the first place, our present pattern and pace are still relatively new: it is in the last few years that we have in effect been reconstituted, and only in the last few weeks that we have found our new home here. So we are, in that sense, already on a new scale of endeavour, that I think is going well at the moment, and gaining momentum. Scholarly activity takes a bit of time to gear up. Secondly, I think it is genuinely difficult to pace the activities of an institution like Gresham College. I see absolutely no virtue in simply becoming another grant-making body, that encourages applications and sifts the merits of other men's ideas; I do not think that would be a very useful way of using our distinguished academic colleagues, although there is absolutely no reason why they should not sponsor an activity which they believe has great merit, and in which they have an interest. There will always be a range of work which the Professors themselves want to follow through or encourage; and our experience so far in developing our 'wider range' activities indicates that there is no shortage of topics. I don't even think we have always to establish a direct link to a specific City of London connection: and if I may give a recent example of this, we supported, with resources and with the coverage of our reputation, the examination and mapping, with new techniques, of the Tomb of Christ.

This Jerusalem Project was worth doing, in and of itself; and that leads on to what is my third part of the answer to 'what happens next'. The added value that we ought to try and give to all of our endeavours is *rigour*. What we do should be well done; the expositions and the arguments must be well conceived, fairly made and reasonably pursued. There may be occasions when we can make a genuinely original contribution or *demarche*; but in all probability I think it is more often likely that we can facilitate, assist and advance an issue that has already been investigated elsewhere. Perhaps we can bring protagonists together, and perhaps we can even get them to listen to each other. It is surprising how often, in public debate, that this does not readily happen. Perhaps we can help to consolidate points of view which have not been put together before. Whatever it is, and whether it is original or entrepreneurial, the fundamental obligation that we continue to owe to the City of London as well as to our Trustees is that it is well done.

There is no shortage of material. In our 'narrower range' of activity there is a wealth of scholarship to be reported and developed by the Gresham Professors, present and future. There is also I hope a chance that we shall be able to develop a way in which former Professors are more easily able to retain their connections with the College, and to be associated with its work. It would be a great pity to ignore the great talents and the affection which we can tap. But, if we look more widely, the rate and the pace of change in the world ensures that, there too, there is no shortage of fascinating, intimidating and even threatening material to draw upon. Indeed so complex and fast-moving has the world become, the place of institutions like Gresham College, that are remote from the market-place and the political jousting ground, can be played down. The immediacy and the scope of practical affairs are indisputably preoccupying: but the decisions which they force upon the players in the game ought to be rooted in much wider considerations – and that is where places like Gresham College have a role to play.

We cannot ignore the fact that the pace of change in the last generation or so has hotted up, to an extent whereby it presents a major challenge in itself. The speed with which we are called upon to adapt to changing circumstances – and values – taxes not only our receptivity but our capacity to balance between what is novel and exciting and what is familiar, and perhaps still good and useful. Novelty is now often a dominant value to so marked an extent that what is familiar may be regarded, by that very fact, as outmoded. This preoccupation with the novel can affect standards, as well as practices: attitudes, as well as institutions.

It used to be said that the British were not very good at this sort of thing: that we hung on to our cosy ways and that the Americans, for example, were much more ready to investigate, and accept, new ideas and methods. We were contrasted in this way to the Japanese, the Germans and almost any other nation one could think of, except perhaps Tibet. This has always been a rather unfair and simplistic generalisation; if you look at the British experience carefully, you find that they do adapt. This has been increasingly true in the last generation. And if you consider how much, in the last 50 years, we have had to face in the way of change, the fashions in which we have managed the challenges have in fact been quite remarkable. There are so many areas in which we have faced up to change, that what is creditable is that in a great many of them we have been able to change the bath-water without throwing out the baby every time. We have, thankfully, never been faced with the extreme requirement of having to change virtually everything at once, and to begin again, virtually with a clean slate, which is what happened to the Germans and the Japanese. This is what is now happening – again – in what, for the moment at least, we still can call the Soviet Union.

There is no doubt that grafting change on to a society that has not faced military defeat and occupation, or total social and economic collapse, is in some ways more complicated than rebuilding from scratch. To have to review everything simplifies at least the problem about what to tackle first. And if the British have sometimes failed to sustain the high rating for cheerful adaptability that I have just awarded them, then their capacity to slow down the rate of change, by having well established and persistent structures and institutions that sometimes provide a refuge is an advantage – which not many other societies enjoy. But sometimes the very resilience of our society has made the progress of change longer, and perhaps more hesitant, than – ideally – it might have been. Ideas and patterns of behaviour take even longer to alter than institutions, and sometimes do hang on persistently. You will remember what Liddell Hart said about generals: that the only thing that took longer, in a general, than getting him to accept a new idea was getting him to give up an old one.

We do perhaps talk more than any other societies do about social compulsions like 'class' and 'tradition'. But not all traditions are pointless; and no other society has been able to rid itself fully of the sorts of distinctions which, in one way or another, replicate our preoccupations with our relative positions in society. If it is still true here, to use the old gibe, that the law is available to all, like the Grill Room at the Ritz, there are equally persistent discriminations in other societies. Some of the most startling and extensive social, occupational and economic discriminations occur in the newest political units of our international system; and what we perhaps ought to make more of is our awareness here, that social justice and economic sufficiency are goals that cannot simply be achieved overnight, and by decree. They need continuous struggle, great determination and a moral code to sustain the fight. We have been at it for at least a hundred and fifty years and there is still a long way to go. But we do as a society have political, social and moral strengths that do sustain the struggle, while they also illustrate that some fundamental, and desirable, changes cannot come about quickly or easily. The grandiloquent ambitions embodied in the slogans of the Russian Revolution have taken 70 years to fail: and it is entirely possible that what these struggling peoples are now trying to do – whatever it is – will take generations more to work through to some sort of equitable stability. Their past offers them no reassurance at all.

The Soviet tragedy is a mighty issue which has all sorts of ramifications for us, on the grandest conceivable scale. If on the one hand it opens up new possibilities for trade, investment and a relaxation of one level of military apprehension, it also confronts us with a novel and perplexing international balance sheet. There used to be a sort of equilibrium, between East and West, with two superpowers managing more or less stable alliances. It was never an easy balance, and it was fraught with potential danger; it has now dribbled away, and is being replaced with something perhaps less dangerous but certainly less predictable. The other problems, which the competition between East and West used often enough to overshadow, are still there. The imbalances between North and South still exist, and there are lots of irritating issues that lie between these cardinal points of the compass.

One of the major causes that led the countries of the European Community to resolve that they should combine together more effectively in a single market, and perhaps a closer sort of political union, was the threat presented by the development of American and Japanese technologies. Whatever now happens in Moscow, or indeed in Maastricht, that challenge has still to be faced. But if things do not go well at Maastricht, remember that the Community has a history of missing the deadlines. The goals that were defined in 1972, to be achieved by 1980, were overthrown by the oil crises of 1973 and 1979; and what has been happening in Eastern Europe perhaps ought to make us think again about what should be done at Maastricht. But we must also remember that the Community has fundamentally to stick to its guns: the goals are more important than any particular time-scale. Even so, we shall all need the Community to sustain a clear vision of what Western Europe's basic interests are. If Eastern Europe is a new problem, resolving the Uruguay Round still has to have weight. If trying to influence the course of events in the Soviet Union now has a new urgency, trying to influence the flux of policy in Washington is still vital.

The Middle East remains a challenge, or rather a series of challenges, with a complexity of a very special intensity. It is still too soon to be sure that Desert Storm was no more than a spectacular military event; it is still too soon to be totally pessimistic about how Arab–Israeli relationships may be conciliated. It is even too soon to be sure that the assertive concept of Muslim awareness is only a political movement. We may find that China, as a fearful bastion of the marxist system, remains in many ways unapproachable. But what may be the most immediate challenges are the reemergence of old rivalries in Eastern Europe and the Soviet Union. We may find that as the Soviet Empire crumbles, the experience of the European decolonisation period in Africa and Asia will be repeated. The impossibility of gratifying all the new expectations quickly or completely will bring instability and anguish. We must dig out the old books and remind ourselves what the Balkan problems were before Hitler and Stalin stamped them under the carpet of repression.

This is a catalogue of woe: not complete, and not particularly starkly drawn. But one of the things we can put into the balance of it is that here in Britain – and indeed in Western Europe generally – we have a heritage of challenge. We simply have to face up to these new difficulties. Life has never been easy; and we have institutions, corporations and experiences that never expected it to be. As an old Whitehall hand, I am inclined to think that our prospects might always be improved by blowing up the Treasury; but in the event that this might not solve all our difficulties (you would have to blow up the Department of Trade and Industry as well ...) we must settle for the tools we have; one of the most important of these is the skill, the resilience and the intelligence of our people, in government, in industry, in commerce and the professions and, indeed, in society as a whole.

We are not in this regard badly placed; but we could always do better, and we must always strive to do so. We are not large enough by ourselves to play any dominating role in international affairs, and even in our new alliances we have no quantitative edge. What we can do is to offer a qualitative contribution that is distinctive. We do it, for example, in the field of defence – but let me make the point here that it has been a long haul. Our forces are very well trained, very experienced, quite well equipped, very well led: and very expensive. Quality does not come cheap. If we want to make the best use of our human resources generally, that will not come cheaply either.

You would, of course, expect a professor to give a puff to education. But the point I want to emphasise is a very general one, that leaves on one side – for the moment – all the structural questions about how we could better organise and more effectively manage the institutions through which the processes of education are condoned. My point is this: high quality education and training is a fundamental asset of great significance – perhaps the most important single attribute of our national infrastructure insofar as it reaches into all other aspects of life, and has immense importance for our social, economic and political well-being. Let me emphasise that education is not only a class-room activity that begins at a set time and ends after a set period of years and depends on teachers. Training is not only a process that produces a particular type of work-force, or results in a piece of paper that signifies a particular level of skill. They are not separate worlds of knowledge or accomplishment, they do not signify simple differences between brain-work and hand-work. They are, together, the way towards understanding, achievement, adaptability and ambition: they are the underpinning of standards of activity and responsibility; and without high standards in education and training, material progress and social well-being will always fall short of the best possible outcome.

It is not a new challenge to face: people have been making the same sort of point at every step along the path of progress – 1868, 1902, 1944, to take the great Education

Acts as illustrative markers. It is right to make the point here in the City, that the setting up of the City and Guilds Institute was another significant milestone. But there is a great deal more to be done; and of course there is a great deal more to it than the incontinent application of additional tax revenues to the existing structures. Nevertheless, in the same way that quality costs, change costs too. The public – and political – assumption that every change is, by definition, a change for the good that will – by implication – save money must be one of the most persistent myths in public life. However, one of the resources that will be called for is public attention and concern. When education and training are seen generally to be crucial public goods, rather than instruments of sectional social advantage, the attention paid to them by institutions, whether political or commercial, is likely to become more thoughtful and enlightened.

Now, let me come to the crunch. Does the existence and activity of Gresham College matter very much in all of this? Do not ask me whether, if Gresham College did not exist, it would be necessary to invent it, because I think that is glib and casuistical. Very few institutions could survive that cynical diversionary tactic. Gresham College does exist, and stands as one example of a belief in the need for wide access to education and knowledge. Whatever Sir Thomas's motives were, in the way he set up this institution, his basic purpose was to spread the new learning. And we follow this lead, four hundred years on.

We can not only exemplify his intentions by our actions; we can carry the argument forward by our advocacy and example. It is really a very worthy cause, and we shall go on trying to do our best to sustain it.

APPENDIX II

ANNUAL SPECIAL LECTURES

1983: HUMAN RIGHTS AND THE DEMOCRATIC
PROCESS
The Rt. Hon. Lord Scarman PC OBE

1984: THE MONARCHY
The Rt. Hon. Lord Blake

1985: THE FALL AND RISE OF THE ENTREPRENEUR
The Rt. Hon. Lord Young of Graffham PC

1987: POPULAR AND UNPOPULAR SCIENCE
Professor Sir George Porter,
President of the Royal Society

1988: RUSSIAN ORTHODOX CHURCH LIFE TODAY -
THE SECOND MILLENNIUM
The Most Reverend Kirill,
Archbishop of Smolensk and Viazma

1989: THE DECLINE OF SOCIALISM
Sir Ralf Dahrendorf KBE FBA
Warden, St. Antony's College, Oxford

1991: SCIENCE AND THEOLOGY; TRAFFIC ACROSS
THE FRONTIER
The Revd. Dr. John Polkinghorne FRS
President of Queens' College, Cambridge

1992: A UNITED GERMANY IN THE NEW EUROPE
H.E. Baron Hermann von Richthofen

1993: THE CITY AND MANUFACTURING INDUSTRY
Howard Davies, Director General, CBI

1994: THE LIFE AND LEGACY OF WILLIAM TYNDALE
The Rt. Revd. and Rt. Hon. The Lord Coggan DD

1995: VE DAY: FIFTY YEARS AFTER
Professor Sir Michael Howard CBE MC

1996: BANKING TODAY
Sir Peter Middleton GCB

1997: SIR THOMAS GRESHAM'S LONDON
Dr. Ian Archer MA DPhil FRHistS

SELECT BIBLIOGRAPHY

Adamson, Ian   'The Foundation and Early History of Gresham
              College' (Univ. of Cambridge PhD thesis 1975).
              'The Administration of Gresham College and its
              Fluctuating Fortunes as a Scientific Institution in
              the Seventeenth Century'
              History of Education ix (1980), 13.
              'The Royal Society and Gresham College
              1660 - 1711', *Royal Society. Notes and Records* 33.

Aubrey, John   *Brief Lives*, ed. Andrew Clark, vol. 1
              (London, 1898).

Becker, Bernard H. *Scientific London* (London, 1874).

Bindoff, S.T.   *The Fame of Sir Thomas Gresham* (London, 1973.
              Neale Lecture in English History 4).

Burgon, J.W.   *The Life and Times of Sir Thomas Gresham*
              (London, 1839).

Colie, Rosalie L. 'Dean Wren's Marginalia and Early Science at
              Oxford', *Bodleian Library Record* vi
              (1960), 541.

Feingold, Mordechai *The Mathematicians' Apprenticeship:
              Science, Universities and Society in England
              1560 - 1640* (Cambridge, 1984).

Forbes, E.G.   (ed) *The Gresham Lectures of John Flamsteed*
              (London, 1975).

Johnson, F.R.   'Gresham College, Precursor of the Royal
                 Society', *Journal of the History of Ideas* I (1940).

Hall, Marie B.   *Promoting Experimental Learning*
                 (Cambridge, 1991).

Hartley, Sir Harold   *The Royal Society, its Origins and Founders*
                 (London, 1991).

Hunter, Michael   *Establishing the New Science*
                 (Woodbridge, 1989).
                 Science and the Shape of Orthodoxy
                 (Woodbridge, 1995).

Saunders, Ann   *The Royal Exchange* (London 1991).
                 (ed) *The Royal Exchange* (London, 1997).
                 'Reconstructing London: a contribution to
                 the Society of Renaissance Studies' Symposium
                 on Gresham College', (London, 1997).

Stow, John   *Survey of the Cities of London and
                 Westminster...*enlarged by John Strype, 2 vols.,
                 (London, 1720).

Taylor, F. Sherwood   'An Early satirical poem on the Royal
                 Society'. *Royal Society. Notes and Records*
                 (October, 1947), 37.

Teague, S.J.   *The City University: a History* (London, 1980).

Ward, John   *Lives of the Professors of Gresham College*
                 (London, 1740).